# POLITICS...
## An Evil Hidden Agenda

Jeanie Cline

# POLITICS...
# An Evil Hidden Agenda

Printed in the United States of America.

Library of Congress Cataloging-Publication Data
Cline, Jeanie
POLITICS...An Evil Hidden Agenda
Pages: 188
Library of Congress Control Number: 2016915301
ISBN-13: 978-1537613512
ISBN-10: 1537613510

"We are in the time of the
Great Awakening on this planet.
The *Light of Truth*, intensifying
with each passing moment,
is nudging many to step forward
and share what they know.
Will such ones follow that nudge
or continue to hide in fear?"
~Eric Jon Phelps ~

*Conspiracy* is a real word for a real event that has existed
in human societies in all cultures through human history.
*Conspiracy Theorists* will question everything, do extensive
research, and come to final conclusions that can really
frighten you! We collaborate with others of like mind and
share theories about everything crucial for others to know.
And, you do have a right to know!

# DEDICATION

To the honorable memory of President John F. Kennedy who stated only seven days before his assassination: *"There's a plot in this country to enslave every man, woman, and child. Before I leave this high and noble office, I intend to expose this plot."* ~ **John F. Kennedy**

(On June 4, 1963, a virtually unknown Presidential decree, *Executive Order 11110*, was signed with the authority to basically strip the Federal Reserve Bank of its power to loan money to the United States Federal Government at interest. With the stroke of a pen, President Kennedy declared that the privately owned Federal Reserve Bank would soon be out of business..."). The *"Kennedy Bucks"* were taken out of circulation two years later.

To the honorable memory of President Abraham Lincoln who was assassinated for the following truths: *"The money powers prey upon the nation in times of peace and conspire against it in times of adversity. The banking powers are more despotic than a monarchy, more insolent than autocracy, more selfish than bureaucracy. They denounce as public enemies all who question their methods or throw light upon their crimes. I have two great enemies - the Southern Army in front of me and the bankers in the rear. Of the two, the one at my rear is my greatest foe. Corporations have been enthroned, and an era of corruption in high places will follow. The money power of the country will endeavor to prolong its reign by working upon the prejudices of the people until the wealth is aggregated in the hands of a few, and the Republic is destroyed."* ~Abraham Lincoln

Both men were elected 100 years apart (Lincoln in 1860, Kennedy in 1960); they were both succeeded by Southerners named Johnson, and the two Johnsons were born 100 years apart (Andrew in 1808, Lyndon in 1908). Both assassins were born 100 years apart (Booth in 1839 and Oswald in 1939) and both died before they could be brought to trial. Lincoln was shot in a theater and his assassin was cornered in a warehouse, while Kennedy was shot from a warehouse and his assassin was captured in a theater. Finally, Lincoln was shot in Ford's Theatre, while Kennedy was shot while riding in a Ford Lincoln, and to top it all off, Kennedy had a secretary named Lincoln (Evelyn Lincoln) while Lincoln had a secretary named Kennedy. The list goes on from there and has been the source of considerable debate ever since.

WHEN THE PEOPLE FEAR THE
GOVERNMENT, THERE IS TYRANNY. WHEN
THE GOVERNMENT FEARS THE PEOPLE,
THERE IS LIBERTY.

*~THOMAS JEFFERSON*

THEY'LL WARN THAT TYRANNY IS
ALWAYS LURKING JUST AROUND THE
CORNER. YOU SHOULD REJECT
THESE VOICES.

*~BARACK OBAMA -2013*

# INTRODUCTION

From Genesis through Revelation in our *Holy Bible*, God has authored his passionate story of love and war and His wrath that will assuredly come in the end. The fallen angel, Lucifer, along with his demonic angels, frequent the earth and create pandemonium in deceiving people with colossal sin in the worst possible form of rebellion. Satan continues to "cause Hell" for the saints in his relentless battle to be equal to God in all authority and power.

In Daniel and Revelation, we read the prophecies and symbolic implications of what is coming at end times through Daniel's vision and John's revelation. Today, Satan uses intellectual, godless, atheistic leaders of world-wide governments masked in secret societies with evil power rapidly spreading across the earth. His political propaganda is to *brainwash* mankind into believing the only solution to the problem of continuous war and bad economy is a one world government – the devil's government of the **New World Order**. Satan's goal is to exercise power and authority over "every tribe, people, language and nation." Satan's authority will be all but unlimited, and almost everyone on Earth will worship him.

Let us not forget that God has sent His Son, Jesus Christ, to bring victory over the evil spirit who has pursued from the beginning of time to receive worship from angels and mankind. Believers in **Jesus** will not worship the Antichrist because they will have their names written *"in the Lamb's Book of Life"* – the book that contains names of all those who have called on the Lamb of God for salvation. Are you ready?

# TABLE OF CONTENTS

## *The Illuminati*

Many people ask is the Illuminati in the Bible and is it real? If the Illuminati conspiracy theory is true, the goal is to bring false doctrine, lies, evil, and demonic influences into the world. When we think about the Illuminati, we think about occult symbols, pyramids, a new world order, and all-seeing eyes.

We think about evil and new agendas being promoted by the media and the entertainment industry. The Illuminati is more than just the media – much more!

What is it? It is a secret society that has infiltrated the government, businesses, banks, and more who seek world domination. These people claim to possess special enlightenment of something that is known only to the organization, such as the Freemasons. They believe there is a "global elite" society that is either in control of the world or is seeking to take control of the world. To summarize, the Illuminati began under the direction of Jesuit priests. Later, a council of five men, one for each of the points on the pentagram, formed what was called, "The Ancient and

Illuminated Seers of Bavaria." They were high order Luciferian Freemasons, thoroughly immersed in mysticism and Eastern mental disciplines, seeking to develop the super powers of the mind. They are the primary motivational forces encouraging global governance, a one-world religious ethic, and centralized control of the world's economic systems. Organizations such as the United Nations, the International Monetary Fund, the World Bank, and the International Criminal Court are seen as tentacles of the Illuminati. They are the driving force behind efforts to brainwash the gullible masses through thought control and manipulation of beliefs, through the press, the educational curriculum, and the political leadership of the nations.

The Illuminati supposedly have a private board of elite, interlocking delegates who control the world's major banks. They create inflations, recessions, and depressions, and manipulate the world markets, supporting certain leaders and coups and undermining others to achieve their overall goals. The supposed goal behind the Illuminati conspiracy is to create and then manage crises that will eventually convince the masses that globalism, with its centralized economic control and one-world religious ethic, is the necessary solution to the world's woes. This structure, usually known as the **"New World Order,"** will, of course, be ruled by the Illuminati.

Does the Illuminati conspiracy have any basis from a Christian/biblical perspective? Perhaps. There are many end-times prophecies in the Bible that are interpreted by most to point to an end-times one-world government, a one-world monetary system, and a one-world religion. Many Bible prophecy interpreters see this **New World Order** (the *old Roman Empire* disguising itself as an organized religion using the **NWO** to regain its "temporal authority" over the world) as being controlled by the Antichrist, the end-times false messiah. If the Illuminati conspiracy and the **New World Order** has any validity and is indeed occurring, for the Christian, there is one fact that must be remembered. God is in control, not the Illuminati. No plan or scheme the Illuminati develop could in any way prevent, or even hinder, God's sovereign plan for the world.

If there is indeed some truth to the Illuminati conspiracy, the Illuminati are nothing but pawns in the hands of Satan, tools to be manipulated in his conflict with God. The fate of the Illuminati will be the same as the fate of their lord – Satan/Lucifer, who will be cast into the lake of fire, to be tormented day and night, forever and ever. Revelation 20:10

In John 16:33 Jesus declared, *"In this world you will have trouble. But take heart! I have overcome the world."*

For Christians, all we need to understand about the Illuminati conspiracy is summarized in the words of 1 John 4:4. *"You dear children, are from God and have overcome them, because the One who is in you is greater than the one who is in the world."*
*(Source: Larry Burkett)*

"The Devil uses men, so it's one group of men versus another group of men, and one path leads to evil, and the true Almighty God leads to goodness. The Illuminati is setting the stage for the antichrist to come."
*(Source: Eric Jon Phelps)*

The following are just a very few of those affiliated with the Illuminati (or those who deceased): New York Post and the medias, Dick Cheney, Walter Cronkite, Alexander Haig, Jack Kemp, Ronald Reagan, Richard M. Nixon, George Bush, Sr., George H. W. Bush, Bill Clinton, Alan Greenspan, Henry

Kissinger, Colin Powell, John Major, William F. Buckley, CIA Director William Casey, Newt Gingrich, David Gergen, and every president with exception of two – Abraham Lincoln and John F. Kennedy.

Presidents: Gerald Ford, Jimmy Carter, Ronald Reagan,
George H.W. Bush, and Richard M. Nixon
(all are members of the **Illuminati**)

## *The Bohemian Grove*

Early July 2011, some of the richest and most powerful men in the world gather at a 2,700 acre campground in Monte Rio, California, for two weeks of heavy drinking, super-secret talks, druid worship (the group insists they are simply "revering the Redwoods"), and other rituals.

Their purpose? To escape the "frontier culture", or uncivilized interests, of common men.

The people that gather at Bohemian Grove - who have included prominent business leaders, former U.S. presidents, musicians, and oil barons – are told that ***"Weaving Spiders Come Not Here,"*** meaning business deals are to be left outside. One exception was in 1942, when a planning for the Manhattan Project took place at the grove, leading to the *creation of the atom bomb.*

A spokesperson for Bohemian Grove stated the people that gather there "share a passion for the outdoors, music, and theater."

The club is so hush-hush that little can be definitively said about it, but much of what we know today is from those who have infiltrated the camp, including Texas-based filmmaker Alex Jones. In 2000, Jones and his cameraman entered the camp with a hidden camera and were able to film a Bohemian Grove ceremony, *'Cremation of the Care'*. During the ceremony, members wear costumes and cremate a coffin effigy called 'Care' before a 40-foot-owl worshipped as **Moloch** (Leviticus 18:21), and in respect to the surrounding Redwood trees. The ceremony involves the poling across a lake of a small boat containing an effigy of Care (called "Dull Care" relating to your worries). Dark, hooded figures receive from the ferryman the image of a human body which is placed on an altar, and, at the end of the ceremony, set on fire. This "cremation" symbolizes that members are banishing the "dull cares" of conscience. The huge Owl Shrine is made of concrete over steel supports. The moss and lichen-covered statue simulates a natural rock formation, yet holds electrical and audio equipment within it. During the ceremony, a recording is used as the voice of The Owl and they call out to the female side of Satan as **she**, and then address the horned god as **he**, which is mixed with the Masonic rites from Scotland. For many years the recorded voice of the owl was that of a club guest, Walter Cronkite. Music and pyrotechnics accompany the ritual for dramatic effect.

Bohemian Grove's spokesperson calls the ceremony *"a traditional musical drama celebrating nature and summertime."* The spokesperson also defended that while he thought Jones' comments to be inaccurate, the footage is real, which can be viewed in its entirety online.

Another infiltrator, *Spy Magazine* writer Philip Weiss, posed as a guest for seven days in 1989, when the waiting list was 33 years long and the grove had several thousand members. Weiss published the article, *Inside Bohemian Grove,* writing: "You know you are inside the Bohemian

Grove when you come down a trail in the woods and hear piano music from amid a group of tents and then round a bend to see a man with a beer in one hand...urinating into the bushes. This is the most gloried-in ritual of the encampment, the freedom of powerful men to pee wherever they like, a right the club has invoked when trying to fight government anti-sex discrimination efforts and one curtailed only when it comes to a few popular redwoods just outside the Dining Circle."

Former President Bill Clinton once responded to a heckler, "The Bohemian club! Did you say Bohemian club? That's where all those rich Republicans go up and stand naked against redwood trees, right? I've never been to the Bohemian club but you oughta go. It'd be good for you. You'd get some fresh air." He has been reported being there many times! The *Sonoma County Free Press*, which has published investigative stories on the grove since at least the 1980's, says activities include plays and comedy shows in which women are portrayed by male actors, and *Lakeside Talks*, in which high-ranking officials speak about information not available to the public. The group calls them *"public interest talks."*

Protests take place at the Bohemian Grove nearly every year. This year's protest is organized by the California State Greens and endorsed by other social activist groups.

Bohemian Grove's 2011 retreat begins in mid-July. We don't suggest any infiltrators try to make their way through the entrance, guarded by camp valets and redwoods some 200 feet in height. It didn't end too well for the last *Vanity Fair* editor who tried it.

*(Source: The Washington Post – 6/15/2011)*

## *The Black Pope*

## The Reverend Father Adolfo Nicolas
*(most powerful man on Earth)*

The First Superior General
*Saint Ignatius of Loyola*
(1541-1556).

**The Superior General of the Society of Jesus** is the official title of the leader of the Society of Jesus – the Roman Catholic religious order, also known as the Jesuits. He is generally addressed as **Father General.** The position sometimes carries the nickname of the **Black Pope**, after his simple black priest's vestments, as contrasted to the white garb of the Pope. The thirtieth and current Superior General is the Reverend Father **Adolfo Nicolas** (2008-current). The first Superior General was Saint **Ignatius of Loyola** (1541-1556).

Black Pope comes partly from the color of the plain black priest' cassock, worn by members of the Society, including the Superior General who is elected for life (although the last two resigned with permission from the pope).

The Superior General is invested with extraordinary power over the members of the Society, higher than the power given to a bishop over the clergy and lay people of a diocese. Jesuit Generals believe in Lucifer and not Satan. They are better known as sorcerers as they dress in black capes and worship Lucifer.

The following is a partial version of **The Extreme Oath of the Jesuits**:

"I furthermore promise and declare that I will, when opportunity presents, make and wage relentless war, secretly or openly, against all heretics, Protestants and Liberals, as I am directed to do, to extirpate and exterminate them from the face of the whole earth; and that I will spare neither age, sex or condition; and that I will hang, waste, boil, flay, strangle and bury alive these infamous heretics, rip up the stomachs and wombs of their women and crush their infants' heads against the walls, in order to annihilate forever their execrable race. That when the same cannot be done openly, I will secretly use the poisoned cup, the strangulating cord, the steel of the poniard or the leaden bullet, regardless of the honor, rank, dignity, or authority of the person or persons, whatever may be their condition in life, either public or private, as I at any time may be directed so to do by any agent of the Pope or Superior of the Brotherhood of the Holy Faith of the Society of Jesus."

This oath appears in its entirety, in the book **"The Suppressed Truth About the Assassination of Abraham**

*Lincoln"* by Burke McCarty, pages 14-16.

Abraham Lincoln was not going to go along with the Fourteenth Amendment which addresses citizenship rights and equal protection of the laws and was proposed in response to issues related to former slaves following the American Civil War. The first section of the Fourteenth Amendment is one of the most litigated parts of the Constitution, forming the basis for landmark decisions such as Roe vs. Wade (1973) regarding abortion, Bush vs. Gore (2000) regarding the 2000 presidential election, and Obergefell vs. Hodges (2015) regarding same-sex marriage. The amendment limits the actions of all state and local officials, including those acting on behalf of such an official.

Abraham Lincoln wanted the Southern states to re-enter the Union on the same footing that they had left, which would have left us with a Federal Republic as Washington had established it. And this, the Jesuits would not allow. It would be converted into an Empire. The states would be subordinate provinces to Washington. And the Fourteenth Amendment would accomplish this with the reversion of citizenship. Lincoln was re-elected and ready to end this, and that is why the Jesuits killed him. Abraham Lincoln had quoted, "The Jesuits never forget, nor forsake."

President John F. Kennedy, the first Roman Catholic to serve in the White house, wanted to end the Vietnam War and also the CIA which is an intelligence arm of the Vatican, the Knights of Malta, and the Jesuits' Federal Reserve Bank. They control all of it. Kennedy sought to resist the temporal power of the Pope in this country and it cost him his life. His son, John F. Kennedy, Jr. wanted to find his father's real killers and he had the power to publish the conclusion of the story; however, they took him out before he could reveal anything.

We must always remember the First Amendment of

our Constitution is *"the Sword of the spirit,"* the Second Amendment is *"the Sword of just defense,"* and the right to bear arms. Most importantly, we must always hold the right to never have our Bible taken from us!

This powerful secret society is comparable to the "Manchurian Candidate" (one who is brainwashed into being an unwitting assassin for a conspiracy). They will kill popes, cardinals, presidents, kings, and Kaisers, to maintain Jesuit power. They are utterly ruthless and, as well, merciless!

The U.S. government uses its military, political, and financial power to maintain the temporal power of the Pope. Believe me, they are everywhere!

The Jesuits made the wars. WWI prepared the land for the people, WWII prepared the people for the land. For us, WWIII will be the battle of Armageddon, which will prepare people for their Messiah – with national repentance while realizing that "Jesus, the Messiah, is the Savior who will deliver them."

There is high-level treason and betrayal of the Jewish race in Israel today, by their own leaders, who are loyal to Rome and the Jesuit Order. An ophthalmology center in Jerusalem run by the Knights of Malta, high-level Freemasonry, and the Jesuit Order are controlling all of Israel.

*(Source: Wikipedia)*


***They will make war against the Lamb, but the Lamb will overcome them because He is Lord of lords and King of kings, and with Him will be His called, chosen and faithful followers.*** **Revelation 17:14**

## *The Rothschild Family ...*

is the wealthiest family on *Earth.* They are estimated to be worth over $350 billion (some say $500 trillion). How, you ask? The central bank in your country is owned and controlled by the Rothschild family. They run the central bank of every country in the entire world. Except for three countries – North Korea, Iran, Cuba. That list used to be longer. In 2002, four other countries were also on that list – Afghanistan, Iraq, Sudan, Libya. How did the Rothschilds gain financial control over those countries? They invaded and infiltrated their land. And with an unlimited amount of money and power, they could manipulate any country into doing it for them. The United States of America was chosen as a puppet to fulfill their plan. They wanted control over Afghanistan and Iraq first. The public couldn't know the real reason behind the invasions. They needed a horrible excuse that would turn America against the Middle East.

*World Trade Center Twin Towers, New York City* – there is a reason people believe 9/11 was an inside job. The U.S. invaded Afghanistan in 2001 and Iraq in 2003. By 2003, both Afghanistan and Iraq's central banks got under control of the Rothschild family – Afghanistan, Iraq, Sudan, Libya. Their first step was complete. Sudan and Libya were Africa's last countries that weren't under their control now. This time they chose the United Nations as their puppet. Certain key people in the UN couldn't resist the money the Rothschild family offered them. (They shall not be named) It changed decisions and interventions taken in certain countries, including Libya and Sudan, where the UN **'intervened'.** By 2011, both Sudan's and Libya's central banks got under control of the Rothschild family – Sudan, Libya. North Korea, Iran and Cuba are their last targets. Who will be their next puppet? They've already chosen. It's already happening around you:

**Iran Supreme Leader sends reply to Obama's letter seeking better relations.**

**U.S. to Restore Full Relations with Cuba.**

Instead of using force, the U.S. is now trying to befriend the countries the Rothschilds want control over. But what about North Korea? (U.S. blames North Korea for **'hack attack'.** The U.S. is unable to befriend North Korea, so they're doing exactly the same as before – trying to make the public turn its back against another country; trying to justify a **'revenge'** attack that's only in place to extend Rothschild's wealth and power on Earth.) *They're manipulating you!* Be vigilant!     *(Source: James Porter)*

### *The Rothschild Banking Dynasty...*

is a family line that has been accused of pulling the political strings of many different governments through their control of various economic systems throughout the world. Historically, there is ample evidence to prove that the family has used its vast fortune to control the political apparatus of numerous nations throughout history, toppling regimes and bringing entire economics to their knees.

### The Rothschild Family has a...

- long line of incest by marrying their cousins in order to prevent losing money and power outside the family.
- Some were very power hungry. Mayer Amschel Rothschild is the founder of the family. He has been quoted as saying, *"Give me control of the economics of a country; and I care not who makes her laws."* They have enough money to set themselves above kings, queens, presidents, prime ministers, and any rulers.
- Since 1919, they had dictated the price of gold and

would appear each morning in the establishment of the Vatican in London and declare the price of gold for that day. In 2004, they gave up that prestigious and powerful position to the Barclay Family.

- U.S. Federal Reserve is a privately owned bank where the U.S. keeps most of its money. One of the major U.S. Federal Reserve Banks is in New York City and it is believed the Rothschild and Rockefeller families have a major say in the U.S. Federal Reserve, which is one of their best kept secrets.

- Many are believed to be **Satanists**. Numerous reports have stated the Rothschild home is always filled with **Satan worshippers.** They have been known to set a spot at the table for the ***Dark Lord*** himself and no one was allowed to sit in his chair. Some family members would sign their name on documents with the *Seal of Solomon* – the symbol of the Jewish people - not the official seal at the time. (see the following graphic diagram). A largely unused symbol only used by magicians and Satanists in previous years.

- They have ties to Secret Societies – the Illuminati and the Freemasons which are the secret underworld and its finances. Following WWI, the Rothschild family was present for the treaty which included their taking over the Bavarian Illuminati founded in 1776.

- They have bankrolled many major wars and control half of the money in the world. They were able to fund most of the major wars over the past 200 years or so, from the Napoleonic War to the World War of the 20th Century. By loaning money to governments with substantial interest instead of loans to individuals, they have been able to become the most powerful family in the history of our world. At the end of each war, the Rothschild family started to see $$$ signs when the loans started coming back, and more money was needed by other countries for their re-building efforts. When the banks were all decimated because of the war, there was only one place to turn, and that was to the Rothschild Family. Perhaps this is why they considered themselves to be above the law in most countries.

- They had very strange parties. In 1972, a photograph appeared to be something out of a *Lady Gaga* video, as some wore big strange animal-style heads and masks with multiple faces. The invitations were written in reverse and required that you would need to see what was penned by holding it in front of a mirror. When arriving at the building, the lights out front were completely red. They also had a strange fascination with bird cages; perhaps due to the reason a family friend was Salvador Dali, a Spanish painter. His quotes were: *"Have no fear of perfection – you'll never reach it! I don't do drugs. I am drugs! Intelligence without ambition is a bird without wings!"*

- They could be hiding up to $650 billion as the world's biggest financial leader. Straying from one lust to another, their assets have become more deluded as some of the family members have chosen to spread the blood line away from the demands of the father's incest and have married outside the Rothschild family. Their net worth is still estimated at probably $1 trillion or greater.

- Nathan Rothschild cheated his way to owning England's finances after the Battle of Waterloo. Through his connections, he was able to get early word that the Battle of Waterloo was not a lost cause. Everyone else figured it would be a loss that would devastate the country. It was believed he went directly to the London Stock Exchange and sold all of his bonds in the British government. When seen doing so, everyone else in the building did the same thing, causing the price to drop to almost nothing. When the prices were at a new low, Nathan bought back all of his bonds as well as those of everyone else who had sold theirs. He gained more power through his evil strategy. (Source: *Ten Dark Secrets – myfirstclasslife.com*)

**Seal of Solomon**

**Baron Nathan Mayer Rothschild**
(of the powerful and wealthy 13 bloodlines)
***Note:*** His right hand inside his vest
represents membership
in the evil secret society of the
**Illuminati**

## *Adolph Hitler*

Maria Anna Schickelgruber became pregnant while living as a common servant girl in a Jewish household. Family members along with peasant farm villagers presumed she was impregnated by the head of the house, Baron Rothschild. However, a Jew by the name of Frankenberger believed he was the baby's father and paid Maria Anna a maintenance allowance for the child's care until he turned fourteen. Believing Frankenberger was his grandfather, this would have made Adolph's father, Alois, half-Jewish and Adolph one-quarter.

Adolph did admit that a Jewish man paid his grandmother money because he had been tricked into believing he was the father of Alois. If true, Adolph's grandmother was having sex with a Jewish man before she became pregnant. When it was discovered, she was banished from the Rothschild, Frankenberger, or Ottenstein home and sent back to her village to have her baby. Funds and "hush money" were secretly provided for her and her son. She paid to keep the paternity a secret.

Alois refused to stay with other peasant farmers in the village of lower Austria, and after settling in Vienna, he became a government official. Apparently he inherited some good traits from his father who was most likely quite the intelligent and successful Jew he had been told.

Alois Schickelgruber was proud of his heritage but found it to his financial advantage to change his name when he turned thirty-nine. Being the shrewd and ambitious man that he was, he had an opportunity to seize the property of one Johann Hiedler who had deceased without any living heirs. Alois made arrangements with the local priest to alter his birth and adoption records, so he scratched out the Schickelgruber name and penciled in "Hiedler". However, he was not so fond of the sound of that named and altered the spelling to "Hitler". Unlike his mother's peasant farmer relatives, he became well-known as an official in the Austrian government. Alois had two sons, Alois, Jr. and Adolph, who were both one-quarter Jewish and three-quarter Nazi-German. It has been said Adolph Hitler was an antichrist.

A memorable quotation by Adolph Hitler is: *"Make the lie big, make it simple, keep saying it, and eventually they will believe it."*

**Adolph Hitler: three-quarter German, one-quarter Jew**

The term, ***antichrist***, refers to the coming final world ruler energized by Satan who will seek to replace and oppose the true Christ. Many antichrists such as Hitler and Napoleon Bonaparte have appeared while this term's first occurrence refers to a particular person prophesied in scripture. This one is plural (false teachers) and refers to many individuals.

Note: Napoleon Bonaparte was quite short in stature and usually posed for portraits with his right hand inserted into the backside of his left lapel. Strangely, I noticed Senator Ted Cruz when appearing on stage during a debate did the very same thing during the Pledge of Allegiance. The other candidates, along with Donald J. Trump, had placed their right hands over their hearts. Cruz's hand-sign was his loyalty and dedication to his membership in the **Illuminati.**

Senator Ted Cruz hiding hand inside jacket
showing dedication to the
**Illuminati.**

**Napoleon Bonaparte –**
**Illuminati** member (thought to be an antichrist)

## *MK-ULTRA*

Following WWII, Nazi scientists were imported to the U.S. in what was known by *Operation Paperclip.* From 1945-1955, almost 1000 German scientists were granted American citizenship – most were Nazi party members who conducted experiments on humans in concentration camps and who had committed other war crimes. Some worked with the CIA, and started NASA. Their work and ideology led to MK-ULTRA.

Most of the human guinea pigs used in such experiments were mental patients, prisoners, drug addicts, and prostitutes or defenseless human beings. To enslave one, the person had to be exposed to torture and treatment methods in order to induce trauma, resulting in becoming dehumanized and broken, ready to be controlled. Through the use of drugs and abuse, the past memory can be altered The project which began in the 50's was kept secret and classified until the late 1970's.

That gives us an idea how powerful are the elite who not only then, but also today, control our world. We are manipulated today. Our political, economic, and cultural lives are *psy ops* (psychological operations). Military operations strategically focus on influencing the enemy's state of mind through non-combative means. We live in an illusion whereby our minds are controlled by the mass media — television, entertainment, music, internet, newspapers, propaganda, and politics. The evil powers that exist try to distract us from knowing about their secrets or societies. When someone learns a rumored secret and publicly announces it, the evil enemy calls it a "conspiracy theory." Many have mysteriously lost their lives by revealing such information or from refusing to adhere to their commands.

The value of history is to remember that nothing is as it seems. It's all being orchestrated and according to a plan that is centuries old. Mankind appears to be edging toward an abyss.

### The Pyramid of Money and Power:

- Queen Elizabeth II — there are two operant Crowns in England, one being Queen Elizabeth II. Although extremely wealthy, the Queen functions largely in a ceremonial capacity and serves to deflect attention away from the other Crown, who issues her marching orders through their control of the English Parliament. The Crown is comprised of a committee of 12 banks headed by the Bank of England (House of Rothschild). They rule the world from the 677 acre, independent sovereign state known as The City of London, or simply "The City". The City is not a part of England, just as Washington, D.C. is not considered a part of the USA and

Virginia and Maryland are referred to as the *Virgin-Mary*. The City is referred to as the wealthiest square mile on Earth and is presided over by a Lord Mayor who is appointed annually. When the Queen wishes to conduct business within the City, she is met by the Lord Mayor at Temple (Templar) Bar where she requests permission to enter this private, sovereign state. She then proceeds into the City walking several paces behind the Mayor. Her entourage may not be clothed in anything other than service uniforms. In the 19th Century, 90% of the world's trade was carried by British ships controlled by the Crown. The other 10% of ships had to pay commissions to the Crown simply for the privilege of using the world's oceans. The Crown reaped billions in profits while operating under the protection of the British armed forces. This was not British commerce or British wealth, but the Crown's commerce and the Crown's wealth. As of 1850, the Rothschild fortune was estimated to be in excess of $10 billion; whereas today, the combined wealth of the banking dynasties is estimated around $500 trillion.

- Council of 13 – these bloodlines are **Astor, Bundy, Collins, DuPont, Freeman, Kennedy, Li, Onassis, Reynolds, Rockefeller, Rothschild, Russell,** and **Van Duyn**. Thirteen families are at the top, and five of these families are the inside core of these thirteen. These 13 families head up the World Government plan and are portrayed as the 13 layers of blocks found on the strange seal on the reverse side of the U.S.

$1 bill. The top Illuminati families are the kingpins in destroying humanity for profit through drug trafficking. Involved in some aspect of the drug trade are **Louis Mortimer Bloomfield, Robert Vesco, Francois Genoud** of **Switzerland, Ivan Slavkov** of Bulgaria, the **Duke of Kent** – Master of the Grand Mother Lodge of the Scottish Rite, and **Jardine Matheson** to mention a few. And we must include all the well-known secret fraternal groups such as the Triads, P2 Masonry, regular Freemasonry, the CIA, the Order of St. John, and the Jesuits.

- Committee of 300 – Also known as *Olympians* are men who know one another, direct the economic destiny of the continent, and choose their successors from their area. *The Knights of the Garter* are the leaders of the Committee of 300. This committee is modeled after the British East India Company's Council of 300, founded by the British aristocracy in 1727. Most of its immense wealth arose out of the opium trade with China. This group is responsible for the phony drug wars here in the U.S. which were to get us to give away our constitutional rights. The committee looks to social convulsions on a global scale, followed by depressions, as a softening-up technique for bigger things to come, as its principal method of creating masses of people all over the world who will become its "welfare" recipients of the future. *They view mankind as being slightly above the level of cattle.* They now call themselves "World Government Founders for the NWO."
- The Round Table *(Think Tanks)* – A world

control group based on freemason lines and has an inner circle who know its precise aims, and an outer circle of "friends" made up of wealthy influential people. Its top members are famous politicians and military leaders. Its funding comes from the infamous house of Rothschild. One of their present power bases is ownership of Reuters-the news agency which supplies a large amount of information to the world media, at which time they can feed any story from their powerful agency to the world's newspapers originating from the Round Table. There are six organizations which have an enormous influence on our daily world: the Council on Foreign Relations, The United Nations, The Bilderberg Group, Club of Rome, Royal Institute of International Affairs, and The Trilateral Commission.

- The Freemason Lodges/Secret Societies – de Poncins wrote: "The great task of freemasonry is to spread ideas sometimes noble and beautiful in appearance but in reality destructive, of which the prototype is the famous motto: Liberty, equality, fraternity. Masonry never works in the full light of the day. Everyone knows of its existence, its meeting places and of many of its adepts, but one is ignorant of its real aims, its real means, its real leaders. The immense majority of masons themselves are in that position. They are only the blind machinery of the secret which they serve... Many honest masons are so blind that they would be stupefied if they knew for what they are being used."

- World Financial Control – The Bank of International Settlements (BIS), Central Banks (US Federal Reserve, Bank of England), International Monetary Fund (IMF), World Bank and Revenue and Taxation organizations (IRS in US, HMRC in UK)
- World Resource Control – organizations which are mainly multinational corporations controlling all sectors including banking, mining, petrochemical, pharmaceutical, communications, computing, manufacturing, supply and delivery, agribusiness, retail and many others. What we are witnessing in all these sectors is a concentration of power and a reduction of competition, corporations are taking over smaller companies and larger companies are merging to the benefit of the corporations and detriment of consumers – less choice and less price competition.
- World Population Control – includes the various agencies that exert control over population either overtly or covertly. Often the people do not even realize they are being controlled and manipulated. These principle methods include: Religion, Advertising and Consumerism, TV and Radio, Celebrity Culture, Employers, Lobby groups and pressure groups, Government (local and national).
- Population Resource – the consumers, workers and debt slaves, the *sheep-people* or chattel. There are roughly 7 billion of us.

The aim of this structure of **shadow government** is believed to be to achieve a dominated first world, an enslaved third world under One World Government – the **NWO.**

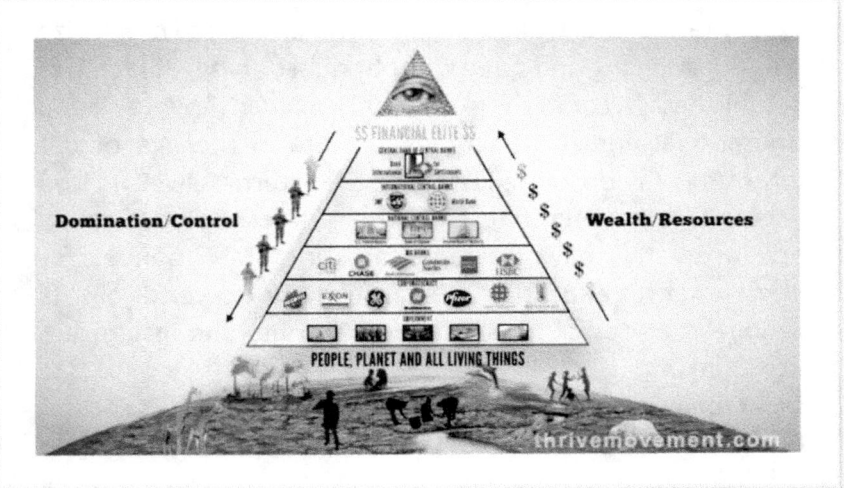

*A Pyramid of Wealth and Power*

<u>Note</u>: Former **President Bill Clinton**, a Rhodes Scholar, is a Bilderberger, a Senior DeMolay (Freemason), and a member of both the CFR and the Trilateral Commission. He joined the Council on Foreign Relations in 1989. Pam Harriman is the person behind Bill Clinton and tied in with the Collins of the satanic group *Hell Fire Club*. Hillary Clinton is known to practice Shamanism witchcraft.
*(Source: theforbiddenknowledge.com)*

***The Brainwashing*** – another mass-enslavement tool that the wealthy and powerful elitists are using against us is the so-called educational system. Schools are no longer what they used to be and children are learning to memorize without thinking and obey without questioning. In fact, this established system is extremely expensive to keep operational and has become obsolete in the age of the internet. Why obsolete? Because the internet gives us free access to almost infinite amounts of information. So why are we still paying huge amounts of money for governmental education? Because these powerful elitists require that our children learn conformity and inside-the-box thinking.

Actually, all of the above combined has a huge impact on our society and the way we think, but their biggest weapon is hands-down, the financial system! And they are bitterly concerned about their greedy money made from our children's **education!**


***Currency Slaves*** – the financial system has stealthily enslaved our species and now we are being used as currency slaves. Many of us work from nine to five every day, in boring and depressing environments, not stimulated by anything creative or constructive.

In most cases, the sole motivation for going to work, is the next paycheck — and no matter how hard we work, we never seem to have enough money. Have you ever wondered why mega-corporations (reaping $billions/year in profits) pay dozens of millions to their CEO's and as close as possible to the minimum wage to the rest of the employees?

This has been carefully designed because a person that is constantly "on the edge," will never have time for self-education, introspection and — eventually — spiritual awakening. Isn't this our main purpose on Earth? To become spiritual beings (and by spiritual, I obviously don't mean religious). The rich and powerful elitists do not need educated people who are capable of critical thinking and have spiritual goals. No! That kind of people are dangerous to the establishment! So, they want obedient "robots," just intelligent enough to operate the machines and keep the system running, but stupid enough never to ask questions.

***Money is the "eye of the devil".*** All of the world's biggest problems have their roots deeply embedded in the financial plague: *wars are profitable, diseases are profitable, Earth's plundering is profitable, human slavery and inhumane working conditions are profitable.*

Our leaders have been corrupted by money and mankind's collective mission on Earth has been hijacked by money. So, why do we need the financial system in the first place? Actually, we do not need it – at least – not anymore! The planet does not charge us a cent for using its natural resources and we have the technology to extract them without physically working all day.

**Note: the single eye (eye of the devil) at the top of the un-finished pyramid of 13 blocks which represent the thirteen bloodlines that control the world.**

## *The Club of Rome*

Founded in 1968, the Club of Rome is a global 'think tank' that deals with a variety of international political issues. According to its website, the Club of Rome is composed of "scientists, economists, businessmen, international high civil servants, heads of state and former heads of state from all five continents who are convinced that the future of humankind is not determined once and for all and that each human being can contribute to the improvement of our societies."

The Ten Kingdoms: The ten regions were established by the United Nations. The Club of Rome was given the task of uniting Europe and dividing the world into manageable blocks. Below is a map of the world, divided into the ten economic regions, which the United Nations and the Club of Rome call "The Ten Kingdoms."

The Club of Rome has been charged with the task of overseeing the regionalization and unification of the entire world; the Club could therefore be said to be one step above the Bilderbergers in the one world hierarchy.

On September 13, 1973, the Club released one such report entitled, "Regionalized and Adaptive Model of the Global World System." The document revealed that the Club had divided the world into ten political/economic regions, which it referred to as "kingdoms". As the ten kingdoms/regions come together, even more in preparation for the reign of the world ruler, we will see the regionalizing of money, then a globalization of monetary exchange or the "cashless society".
**(Revelation 13)**

Regarding the world and its division into economic regions, here are countries for each region:

1. ***NAFTA*** – America, Canada, Mexico
2. ***European Union*** – Western Europe as a whole region
3. Japan
4. Australia, New Zealand, South Africa
5. Eastern Europe, Pakistan, Afghanistan, Russia, and former Soviet Union countries
6. Central and South America, Cuba, Caribbean Islands
7. The Middle East and North Africa
8. The rest of Africa, except South Africa
9. South and Southeast Asia, India
10. China (including Mongolia) The islands of the seas fit in with the closest region

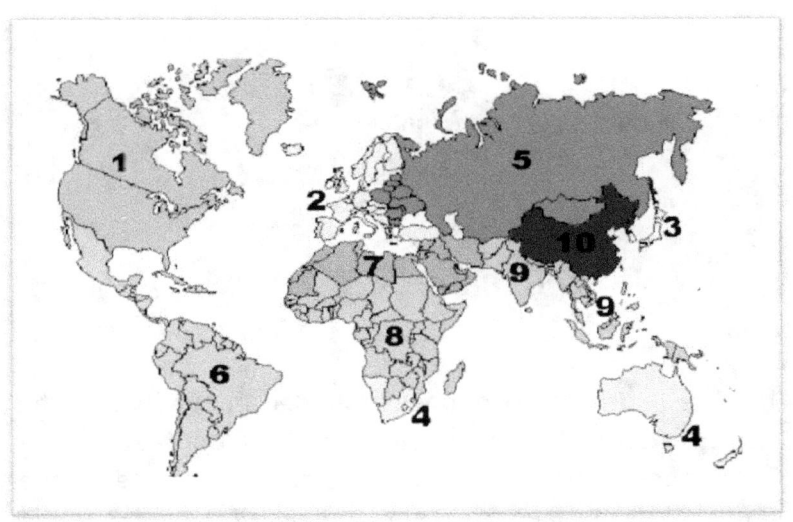

## The Future Ten Economic Regions of the World

## *The Bilderberg Group*

The Bilderberg Group was founded in 1954 when the most powerful men in the world met for the first time in Oosterbeek, Netherlands and debated the future of the world. They decided to meet annually in secret to help foster dialogue between Europe and North America. They hold a membership of at least 150 political leaders and experts from industry, finance, academia, and the media. They are world power elites mostly from America, Canada, and Western Europe with familiar names like David Rockefeller, Henry Kissinger, Bill Clinton, Gordon Brown, Angela Merkel, Alan Greenspan, Ben Bernanke, Larry Summers, Tim Geithner, Lloyd Blankfein, George Soros, Donald Rumsfield, Rupert Murdoch, other heads of state, influential senators, congressmen and parliamentarians, Pentagon and NATO brass, members of European royalty, selected media figures, and invited others – some quietly by some accounts like Barack Obama and many of his top officials.

**Former U.S. Secretary of State and political mastermind, Dr. Henry Kissinger, is one of the most influential participants at the annual Bilderberg meetings.**

Early in its history, Bilderbergers decided *to create an* *'Aristocracy of Purpose' between Europe and the U.S.* <u>to reach consensus to rule the world on matters of *policy, economics, and overall strategy*</u>. **NATO** *was essential for their plans – to ensure "perpetual war and nuclear blackmail" to be used as necessary; then proceed to loot the planet, achieve fabulous wealth and power, and crush all challengers to keep it.*

Bilderbergers comprise the world's most exclusive club. No one buys their way in. Only the *Group's Steering Committee* decides whom to invite, and in all cases participants are adherents to **One World Order** governance run by top power elites.

Arkansas governor **Bill Clinton** who attended in 1991 was informed by David Rockefeller why the North American

Free Trade Agreement was a Bilderberg priority and that the group needed him to support it. The next year Clinton was elected president, and then on January 1, 1994, **NAFTA** took effect. Numerous other examples are similar, including who gets chosen for powerful government, military, and other key positions.

**The original conference was held at the Hotel de Bilderberg in Oosterbeek, Netherlands from May 29-31, 1954**

The Group's grand design is for a ***One World Government*** (**World Company**) with a single, global marketplace, policed by one world army, and financially regulated by one ***World (Central) Bank*** using one global currency.
*(Source: Age of Truth)*

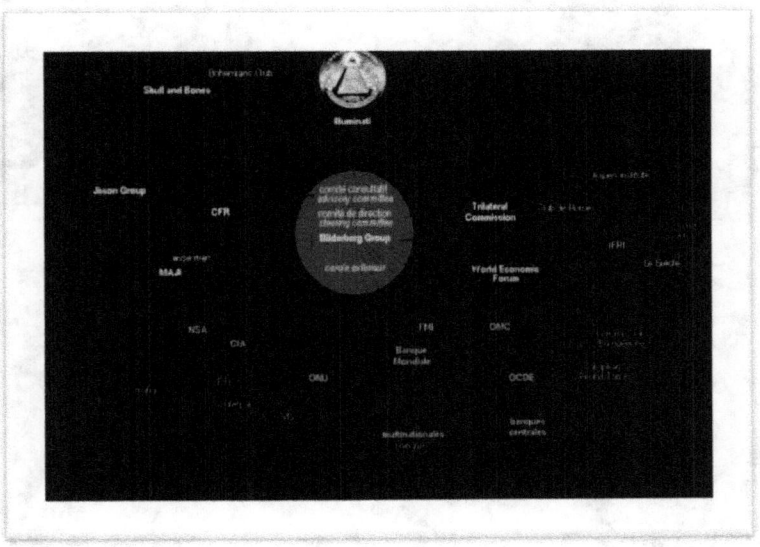

**Illuminati, Bilderberg Group, Bohemian Club, Skull and Bones, Jason Group, CFR, MAJI, NSA, CIA, FBI, ONU and foreign country secret societies**

**David Rockefeller, one of the most significant founders and participants of the Bilderberg Group.**

**Heads of state – Tony Blair, George W. Bush, Jacques, Chirac, Silvio Berlusconi, Vladimir Putin – Elite participants of the Bilderberg Group**

**Bill Gates is a Bilderberger.**

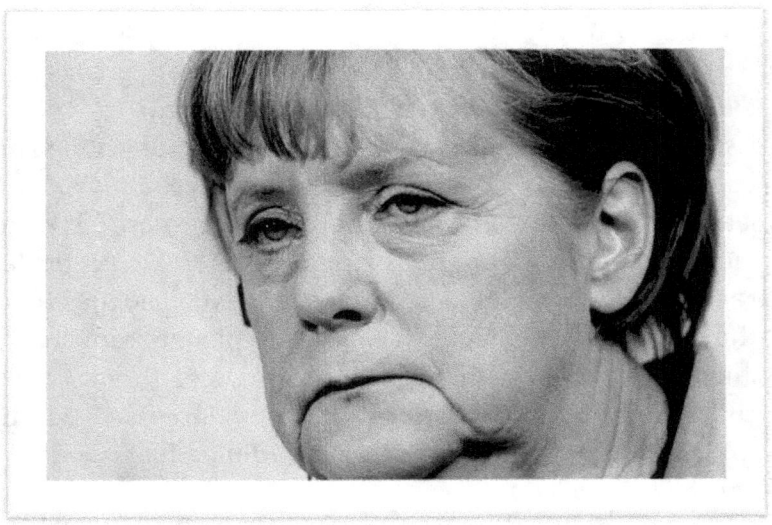

**German Chancellor Angela Merkel is a Bilderberger.**

# The Trilateral Commission

*The Trilateral Commission* is a non-governmental, non-partisan discussion group founded by David Rockefeller in July 1973. He was one of the Bilderbergers who made Professor Zbigniew Brzezinski the Chairman and co-founder.

The Commission states their goal is to bring together experienced leaders within the private sector to discuss issues of global concern at a time when communication and cooperation between Europe, North America, and Asia are lacking. They state they have grown since early days to include members from more countries in these particular regions, and continue to find that study and dialogue about the pressing problems facing our planet remain as important today as in 1973. Problems and threats have changed, but their importance has only increased due to the more interconnected and interdependent world in which we now live.

Some past members have included Dick Cheney, William Cohen, Dianne Feinstein, David Gergen, and Henry

Kissinger, and also, former Presidents George H.W. Bush, Jimmy Carter, and Bill Clinton.

Actions taken by the Trilateral Commission largely help the banking industry. Private multinational banks, particularly Rockefeller's Chase Manhattan, have loaned nearly $52 billion to developing countries. There is increasing evidence of a plan underway to corner the global supply of gold which will lay the groundwork for a global currency exclusively controlled by the Trilateral and their friends. *(Source: Jeremiah Project)*

Journalist **Bill Moyers** (a CFR member), wrote about the power of **David Rockefeller** in 1980: *"David Rockefeller is the most conspicuous representative today of the ruling class, a multinational fraternity of men who shape the global economy and manage the flow of its capital...Private citizen David Rockefeller is accorded privileges of a head of state...He is untouched by customs or passport offices and hardly pauses for traffic lights."*

**Senator Barry Goldwater** wrote in his book, <u>With No Apologies:</u> *"In my view, the Trilateral Commission represents a skillful, coordinated effort to seize control and consolidate the four centers of power: political, monetary, intellectual, and ecclesiastical. All this is to be done in the interest of creating a more peaceful, more productive world community. What the Trilateralists truly intend is the creation of a worldwide economic power superior to the political governments of the nation-states involved. They believe the abundant materialism they propose to create will overwhelm existing differences. As managers and creators of the system they will rule the future."*

In the July 1977 issue of <u>Atlantic Monthly</u>, Jeremiah Novak wrote: *"Although the Commission's primary concern is economic, the Trilateralists pinpointed a vital political objective: to gain control of the American Presidency...For the third time in this century, a group including American schools, businessmen, and government officials is planning to fashion a new world order.."*

Craig S. Karpel wrote in a November 1977, <u>Penthouse</u> magazine article ***Cartergate: The Death of Democracy:*** *"The presidency of the United States and the key cabinet departments of the federal government have been taken over by a private organization dedicated to the subordination of the domestic interests of the United States to the international interests of the multi-national banks and corporations. It would be unfair to say that the Trilateral Commission dominates the Carter Administration – the Trilateral Commission **is** the Carter Administration."*

# The JASON Group,

# JASON Scholars,

# JASON Society

**Jason** was an ancient Greek mythological hero who was famous for his role as the leader of the Argonauts and their quest for the Golden Fleece. He was the son of Aeson, the rightful king of Lolcos. He was married to the sorceress Medea. (Wikipedia)

The secret society, the JASON Society (or JASON Scholars), takes its name from this story, and is a branch of the Order of the Quest – one of the highest degrees in the Illuminati above the Skull and Bones and the Scroll and Key. The golden fleece has the role of truth to the JASON members. Jason represents the search for truth; therefore, the name JASON Society represents a group of men who are engaged in a search for the truth. The name Jason is spelled with capital letters when used as the name of the JASON

Society and lower-case letters are never used when referring to this secret group. It has been reported that President Dwight Eisenhower had commissioned the JASON Society to examine all of the evidence, facts, lies and deception, and find the truth of the *"alien question."*

The JASON Group (not the same as JASON Society) include members of the famous Manhattan Project, which brought together almost every leading physicist in the nation to build the atomic bomb during WWII. No leaks have ever occurred within this highly discreet civilian group and the JASON name never appears in documents which may come under public scrutiny. The JASON Group is a scientific organization formed and hired by the JASON Society and the U.S. Government for obvious reasons. *(Source: Angel Fire)*

Allegedly former President Dwight Eisenhower commissioned the JASON Society under the leadership of Allen Welsh Dulles, Dr. Zbigniew Brzezinski, and Dr. Henry Kissinger. The society was made up of thirty-two of the most prominent men in the U.S.A.

MJ-12 allegedly operates inside the JASON Society. The top twelve members of the JASON Society were designated as MJ-12 and have control of everything. The actual cost of funding the Alien connected projects is higher than anything you could imagine. Some believe the MJ-12 runs most of the world's illegal drug trade to hide funding and thus keep the secret from congress and the people of the U.S. It was justified in that it would identify and eliminate the weak and undesired elements of our society.

A secret meeting place was constructed for the MJ-12 group in Maryland and is only accessible by air. It contains full living, recreational, and other facilities for the group and the JASON Society. It is code named *"The Country Club"*. The land was donated by the Rockefeller family. Only those with

Ultra Top Secret – MAJI (Majority Agency for Joint Intelligence) clearances are allowed to attend. *(Source: Crystal Links)*

## *The Skull and Bones*

The most famous secret society in America which was co-founded by Attorney General Alphonso Taft at Yale in 1832, the father of future president, William Howard Taft, is The Skull and Bones.

It is believed that Yale junior class members are tapped for membership each fall by some measure of leadership, influence and breeding. Among the business titans, poets, and politicians, three are U.S. Presidents.

In the class of 1916, Prescott Bush, the grandfather of "Dubya" was thought to be quite the man at Yale. He was reported to have dug up and absconded with the skull of the legendary Native American warrior Geronimo during WWI. However, legend has it that Geronimo's head is still inside Skull and Bones HQ known as "The Tomb," at 64 High Street in New Haven.

Robert Lovett, class of 1918, was the flawless Bonesman insider. He went on to become Harry Truman's Secretary of War and the man whom many have called *"The Architect of The Cold War"*. Along with sharing a membership timeline with Prescott Bush, Lovett was also friendly with fellow Bonesman Harvey Hollister Bundy who served with Lovett in Truman's War Cabinet and was the father of future Bonesman McGeorge Bundy. The Bundy families are in the Council of 13 that head up the World Government Plan.

Before becoming one of JFK's "Wise Men," Bundy was another Bonesman with a long family lineage of getting "tapped" for the society. He had a personality all his own and his pals nicknamed him, "Odin" (head god in Norse mythology).

The second ever Bonesman to be elected President, George Herbert Walker Bush ("41") was also a fighter pilot in WWII, Ambassador to "Red China", and Director of the CIA. His training at Skull and Bones must have been invaluable in the career he made out of keeping safe the secrets of the state.

Class of 1950, William F. Buckley, Jr. was "tapped" for The Skull and Bones.

John F. Kerry, class of 1966, and is today the 68th Secretary of State was a college junior when he was "tapped."

George W. Bush ("W") was a man whose family was synonymous with The Skull and Bones by the time he arrived on Yale's campus as a Freshman but it has been whispered that many thought his family would agree as to his not being "tapped" since George was a rather "distractible" young man. But after joining up, he became the third Bonesman to occupy the office of the President in the White House.

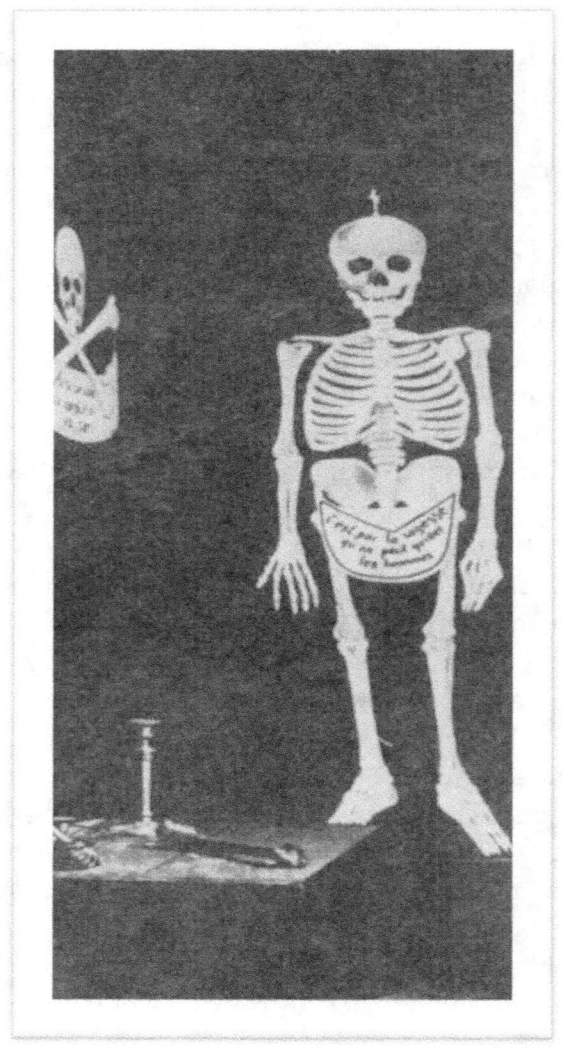

**The Skull and Bones Secret Society at
Yale University**

To sum it up, The Skull and Bones secret society consists of members who believe in the ancient rituals of the occults which operate by offering sacrifices – humans and animals. They believe they receive the power of those departed souls which "enter" them upon their death, and take part in ceremonies where they drink human blood and eat human flesh.

They also believe in opening portals between other dimensions and practice ancient and satanic rituals to reach a **New World Order** – of course with The Rothschild, The Rockefeller, and the rest of the 13 bloodlines at its pinnacle.

Yes, I truly admit this is something you normally do not read about or talk about with any rational thought. However, as freakish as it may be, it must be working for all the secret societies or they would not have remained religiously involved for centuries.

When Saddam Hussein talked of *'the devil Bush'*, he may not have been so far from the truth since three generations of the Bush clan are proven initiates of this multi-general occult lodge. Undergraduates found that the *'holy of holies'* inner sanctum has red velvet walls and carpet, with a large pentagram emblazoned on the wall.

Geronimo's burial marker, where, apparently, six army officers – alumni of Yale and members of the Skull and Bones Society – plundered the grave.

## *Who Are the Zionists?*

Zionism is a movement founded by Theodor Herzl in 1896 whose goal was the return of Jews to Zion, Jerusalem, and the Land of Israel. Zionism comes from Zion, the hill on which the Temple of Jerusalem was situated. Supporters of this movement are called "Zionists."

Baron Edmond Rothschild of Paris, the managing partner of the original M.A. Rothschild & Son banking firm was the main support of the Zionist political movement from the beginning. He was known as the father of Jewish colonization in Palestine. The Rothschilds wanted the minerals of Palestine. They knew about the fabulous mineral wealth of the Dead Sea estimated at five trillion dollars and they had taken steps to acquire it.

It was only when Theodor Herzl, Austrian journalist and playwright, decided to sell Lord Rothschild his colonization scheme – his plan of conquest – that the Rothschild family took over the financing and management of Herzl's Zionist World Empire and Herzl became their lieutenant. Herzl had previously met with the Sultan of Turkey and offered him five million dollars for the purchase of Palestine, in which he told him he would gather the Jews and they would safely be colonized in Palestine. The Sultan was excited over Herzl's proposal and the great sum of money was an enticement. The only problem for Herzl was that he needed the funds to complete the transaction.

That was in 1898 and Theodor Herzl, 'father of Political Zionism,' is now dead; however, the perpetual Rothschild partnership never dies and they now control the gold, the press, and the economy of the people of the world.

Herzl had quoted in his journal:

> *"He that cries Hosanna for you today,*
> *Tomorrow will cry: Crucify!"*

The mineral wealth of Palestine belongs to the Allies of WWI by right of conquest. It did not belong to the British who were only its custodians by virtue of a mandate. The Zionists stole these minerals by the newly created and recognized state of Israel.

We need the minerals for our national defense and need to recover them for the use and benefit of ourselves and our Allies of WWI. The recovery of these minerals together with the destruction of the Zionists would establish peace in our world – a permanent peace. There is no other way. The Rothschilds should be banished and their ill-gotten wealth confiscated and devoted to the public good.

*(Source: BibleBelievers.org)*


Zionist forces have control over USA politics, military, and foreign policy. **The National Security Agency raw data** (unfiltered information on individual Americans that should be covered by privacy) **goes directly to Tel Aviv.**

## *The Dome of the Rock*

In order to remove the Dome of the Rock sitting on the Temple (which the Jesuits want to happen), the Jesuit General would somehow, some way, make American bombers do it, which would create hatred for our nation of the United States. Their reason is because there are more Protestants and more Jews in the U.S. than in any country in the world. They want to kill all of those people – so what better way than to create a Jihad, a Moslem fanatical attack against the U.S., coupled with a Chinese invasion from the East.

The Jews are not going to destroy the Temple site, because if they do, Rome will destroy their efforts of re-building the Temple. If Moslems control all of Jerusalem, the Temple will never be re-built. It has to stay in Jewish hands because the Jews need their own homeland. They're entitled to the nation and their own Temple of Worship.

But what they don't know is that they are being used by the Jesuits to re-build their own Temple, that they would love to have re-built, for the Pope so he can sit there and be the man of sin, the antichrist of the Book of Daniel, Chapter 9.

Anyone who is going to resist the Jesuit Order must be doing it as a matter of a *"religious conviction"*, being protected by God and good men who are loyal to Him. If it's simply political with a hired Secret Service, you can forget it! *You are dead!*

The nation of Islam was founded in Chicago and under Jesuit control. Their army will start agitation and with their millions of rounds stored in all the major cities with guns stored everywhere, they can start the race war against Protestants and Jews. When that happens, Washington will suspend the Second Amendment of the Constitution and implement Martial Law, and the Jesuits will have what they want.

They use the Blacks in the North who hate the White people for their own destruction, and destruction of the Black people themselves. And the nation of Islam is part of that war. The Jesuits know their strength and weaknesses since they are masters of the races – both black and white.

To sum it all up, men of God can tell the truth or sit back and let the Jesuits advocate everyone giving up, laying down their guns, and submitting to the **New World Order**, under the **Pope.**

*Eric Jon Phelps  (The Spectrum)*

*If a ruler listens to lies, all his officials become wicked.* **Proverbs 29:12**

## *Global Warming and Hydrogen Bomb*

Edward Teller (1908-2003) was a well-known physicist and held the reputation as *"father of the hydrogen bomb"*. His close friend was Robert Oppenheimer who was born in Hungary and the son of a Jewish man. He emigrated to the United States and was our government's foremost scientific advisor.

A famed historian, Richard Rhodes, had once publicly stated, "Teller has consistently given bad advice to every president that he has worked for." Earlier when Teller migrated to Germany, England and America, he saw the noose of Nazism tightening around Europe. This brought about the cruelties of communism and Nazism which seems to have dictated almost every one of Teller's major decisions for the rest of his life. The fear of dictatorship manifested itself early, leading Teller to be among the first ones to push for a US nuclear weapons program. He lobbied vigorously for the government to be aware of a potential German atomic project. Whenever the war started, he was a respected professor at George Washington University and became one of Robert Oppenheimer's first recruits at Los Alamos where he moved at the beginning of the Manhattan Project in the spring of 1943. Their personalities clashed at the beginning – both brilliant physicists, with Teller having the mistrust.

**Dr. Edward Teller**
**"Father of the Hydrogen Bomb"**

After the war, Teller kept on pushing for the hydrogen bomb while receiving support from scientists, politicians and the military. Sadly his initial design for the Super was fatally flawed. However, knowing this he continued taking advantage of the worsening political situation and his prominence in the scientific community; thus, creating his first dishonest act.

His second dishonest act was withholding credit from the man who actually came up with the first successful idea for a hydrogen bomb – Stanislaw Ulam. He was a brilliant mathematician who performed detailed calculations which revealed errors in Teller's original Super design. When Teller saw the merit of his idea, he significantly refined it. Since then almost every hydrogen bomb in the world's nuclear arsenals has been constructed on the basis of the Teller-Ulam model. However, Teller continued to deny Ulam the credit for the idea even in his later years.

Scientists and governments refer to, what is commonly known around the world as Chemtrails (not to be confused with normal jet contrails), as Stratospheric Aerosol Geo-engineering or S.A.G. It has been documented as far back as the late 1980's that the U.S. Government has been conducting covert S.A.G. programs. These covert operations are now being conducted worldwide throughout the U.S. and N.A.T.O. countries on an on-going daily basis. This program is a global covert operation.

Edward Teller, famed scientist, when working at Lawrence Livermore National Laboratory in Livermore, California, was the co-inventor of the Hydrogen Bomb as previously mentioned. He was the first scientist who came up with the theory if you sprayed metallic particulates in the upper atmosphere you could cool the Earth. He was reported to have tried to obtain funding for researching his theory but was unsuccessful.

In 1952, the founders of the new Livermore branch of the University of California Radiation Laboratory are shown: E. O. Lawrence, Teller, and Herbert F. York, the first director.

**Dr. Edward Teller and laboratory director, Herbert F. York**

It is now apparent that the U.S. government has implemented Teller's theory by spraying megatons of particulate heavy metals and chemicals like aluminum, barium, strontium and sulfur hexafluoride into the stratosphere.

In 1991, a U.S. patent was issued to Hughes Aircraft Company; the Stratospheric Welsbach Seeding For Reduction of Global Warming Patent #5,003,186. It proposed injecting into the upper atmosphere, a "very fine, white talcum-like" powder of aluminum oxide, barium oxide and other oxides for the stated purpose of reducing Global Warming.

On October 2, 2001, Rep. Dennis Kucinich introduced the "Space Preservation Act of 2001 (HR 2977), which called for the elimination of "exotic weaponry" from space. Among the weapons to be banned were *"weather modifying weapons such as...chemtrails."* Though it was later amended to remove the word chemtrails, the original bill acknowledging this technology remains on the pages of the Congressional Record.

Aluminum and barium are being found in dangerous levels in water and soil samples taken nationwide. Respiratory and neurological illnesses have risen dramatically and asthma is near epidemic levels in children. Numerous studies have connected aluminum exposure to neurological damage (like Alzheimer's) and a host of other diseases. Other related diseases such as chronic fatigue syndrome, fibromyalgia and multiple-chemical sensitivities have steadily risen since the deployment of these on-going programs.

The low-dose, long-term, exposure to these toxic chemicals and heavy metals has a devastating effect on our health by destroying our immune system and making people more vulnerable to disease and critical/chronic illnesses. Recent heavy metal testing shows off-the-chart ranges of toxic chemicals and heavy metals like aluminum and barium in young children.

The content of the fallout from these aerosols includes fibers, metal particulates and biological elements which have been detected through environmental testing. These micro-particles enter into our bodies and weaken our immune system, making us more acceptable to chronic illnesses both physically and psychologically.

"Stratospheric aerosols", are proposed by Geo-scientists, as a way to manage solar radiation and climate change by aerosol spraying fine particulates into our upper atmosphere. It also reduces solar intake as much as 70% on heavy spray days. This is caused because the man-made clouds and the sky shield block the sunlight.

The U.S. military has openly stated that it is their goal to *"OWN THE WEATHER"* by 2025. They are capable of affecting and controlling storms and the Earth's electrical balance. They can manipulate radio frequencies and the electromagnetic spectrum for military and surveillance purposes. ***They can alter human awareness and behavior. Deborah J. Whitman, Pres.***

*(Source: Environmental Voices)*

## *Operation Majestic-12*

The Top Secret *Operation Majestic-12* (group consisting of twelve members) was established by order of President Harry S. Truman in 1947. It was created to take charge of the technical, sociological and other aspects of the crashed UFO's and the small alien occupants, dead or alive, that were recovered. In later years this operation evolved into and became known as MAJI (the Majority Agency for Joint Intelligence). MAJI is the most secret of all intelligence groups and out-ranks all other intelligence agencies including the National Security Agency (NSA) and the Central Intelligence Agency (CIA). MAJI is responsible directly and "only" to the President of the United States.

In 1954, President Dwight D. Eisenhower established a permanent committee to be known as <u>Majority Twelve</u> to oversee and conduct all covert activities concerned with the alien question, and those were: Nelson Rockefeller, CIA Director Allen Welsh Dulles, Secretary of State John Foster Dulles, Secretary of Defense Charles E. Wilson, Admiral Arthur W. Radford, FBI Director J. Edgar Hoover, and six men from the Council on Foreign Relations known as the *"Wise Men."* These men were all members of a secret society of scholars that called themselves *"The Jason Society"* or *"The Jason Scholars"* who recruited their members from the *"The Skull and Bones"* and the *"Scroll and Key"* societies of Harvard and Yale. The "Wise Men" were key members of the Council on Foreign Relations and among them were Gordon Dean, George Bush, and Zbigniew Brzezinski.

MAJI and the U.S. government have in its possession spaceships manufactured on other planets, as well as the occupants of those interstellar crafts. And, that since 1964, they have maintained radio contact with the aliens through Project Sigma.

*(Source: The Ultimate Secret/Wikipedia)*

**President Harry S. Truman,
Millennial Freemason**

TOP SECRET
EYES ONLY
THE WHITE HOUSE
WASHINGTON

September 24, 1947.

MEMORANDUM FOR THE SECRETARY OF DEFENSE

Dear Secretary Forrestal:

As per our recent conversation on this matter, you are hereby authorized to proceed with all due speed and caution upon your undertaking. Hereafter this matter shall be referred to only as Operation Majestic Twelve.

It continues to be my feeling that any future considerations relative to the ultimate disposition of this matter should rest solely with the Office of the President following appropriate discussions with yourself, Dr. Bush and the Director of Central Intelligence.

President Harry Truman - The Secret of the UFO Program.

Source: www.crystalinks.com

*What if I told you....*
*there are multiple cures*
*for cancer,*
*but they're hidden in a*
*huge vault since*
*cancer is worth*
*$160 billion a year!*

## *Shriner Masons and Muslims*

The Masons are especially strong in the U.S. but only weakly represented in Europe. However, they may have stronger helpers: *The Muslim Brotherhood.*

In high Freemasonry, oaths are secretly sworn on the Koran. Many American presidents were Shriners and also wore the Shriner Hat. Today that is no longer officially supported. With Barack Obama, there was a slip of the tongue at the swearing ceremony, so the oath had to be carried out again behind closed doors. It's possible the Koran was there the second time. Also in the speech of Reverend Warren before the swearing, the name of Jesus was named by his Islamic name of Isa.

Shriner lodges have hats with different names, not any hat wearing the name of "Ararat." But each hat has the five-pointed star, the crescent and the sword. These are all Islamic symbols. No other proof is needed that the violent Islam is indulged. Some hats have the Sphinx.

The Shriners are a high level of Freemasonry. The Arabic writing on a Shriners mosque means, *"No god but Allah."*

The star and crescent are the symbol of the Ottoman Empire (Turkish empire) and Mount Ararat is located in Turkey. Biblically, Turkey also has a central role, and the seat of Satan is pinpointed in Turkey. In Arabic, the Sphinx is called Abu al-Hol (Father of Terror). Also it is no meaningless coincidence that the Sphinx is depicted in many Shriner symbols. I believe this reasons why any criticism of Islam is being stifled by (Masonic) men of the state and clergy as *"racist"* or *"Islamophobic."* It is as if the masters of the world want to establish Islam and let it creep in and destroy the good Christian culture. It is calculus and Islamic war strategy with the migration weapon.

The lower Freemasons have no idea that the High Shriner Freemasons are working for the Jesuit General due to Mason Fredrick the Great of Prussia, who wrote the High Degrees, the last 8 Degrees, of the Scottish Rite Freemasonry, in 1773. All Shriners must be Masons and a man is a fully accepted "Blue Lodge" Mason after he has received and proved proficiency in the first three degrees. The Membership-slogan is **Together We Can** and President Obama's motto is **"Yes We Can!"**

President Obama's brother, Malik, is an important member of the Muslim Brotherhood and according to an Egyptian paper, US Muslim, President Obama is a full member of the Muslim Brotherhood also. The Muslim Brotherhood's strategic plan, the group's mission in America, is a "civilization-jihadist process...a kind of grand jihad in eliminating and destroying Western civilization from within" by our hands.

Shriner's Oath: Candidates for induction into the Shriners are greeted by a High Priest, who says: *"By the existence of Allah and the creed of Mohammed; by the legendary sanctify of our Tabernacle at Mecca, we greet you."* The inductees then swear on the Bible and the Koran,

80

in the name of Mohammed, and invoke Masonry's usual gruesome penalties upon themselves:

*"I do hereby, upon this Bible, and on the mysterious legend of the Koran, and its dedication to the Mohammedan faith, promise and swear and vow...that I will never reveal any secret part or portion whatsoever of the ceremonies...and now upon this sacred book, by the sincerity of a Moslem's oath I here register this irrevocable vow...in willful violation whereof may I incur the fearful penalty of having my eyeballs pierced to the center with a three-edged blade, my feet flayed and I be forced to walk the hot sands upon the sterile shores of the Red Sea until the flaming sun shall strike me with livid plague, and may Allah, the god of Arab, Moslem and Mohammedan, the god of our fathers, support me to the entire fulfillment of the same. Amen. Amen. Amen."*

With this oath, Christians swear on the Koran, and declare Allah to be "the god of our fathers." (*Source: Excerpt from The Origins and Influence of Masonry by Lee Penn, SCP Journal, Berkeley, California*)

## *The Knights of Malta*

The full name of The Knights of Malta is ***The Sovereign Military Hospitaller Order of Saint John of Jerusalem of Rhodes and Malta.*** The Sovereign order of Malta is real contrary to conspiracy theory. The organization provides humanitarian assistance in 120 countries and diplomatic relations with 104 countries.

This Order is one of the most ancient Catholic religious orders in the world. Its pedigree dates back to around 1048 or 1050, when the Caliph of Egypt gave a group of merchants from Amalfi permission to build a combination church, hospital and convent in Jerusalem, with the understanding that the hospital would admit pilgrims of all religions and races.

In 1113, Pope Paschal, II issued a bull placing the Order under the authority of the Holy See, and also giving the right to elect its leaders without interference from other authorities, whether secular or religious. Since the Crusades were (to say the least) a bloody, violent time, the Order eventually acquired a military bent as it defended patients, pilgrims and conquered territory from Muslim forces.

These two abilities − the independence from other nations and the right to use military force − provide the basis for the Order's peculiar standing in the international community.

It's no secret that the Order had problems over the course of its centuries-old existence. In 1291, prompted by the fall of the last Christian compound in the area, the Order struck out for the island of Cyprus. From there the Order relocated to Rhodes where it built one of the most powerful naval forces in the Mediterranean. The Order called Rhodes home until 1523, and during this time it issued its own currency and cultivated diplomatic relationships with other countries. When Sultan Suleiman (the Magnificent) held the Order under siege for months, the knights were eventually forced to surrender the island.

For seven years the Order was a sovereign entity with no territory of its own. Fortunately, Emperor Charles, V gifted the island of Malta to the Order in 1530. This lasted until 1798, when Napoleon took over the island. By this point the Order had a long-standing rule forbidding its forces from raising arms against other Christians. As a result, they left Malta, traveling through Messina, Catania and Ferrara before eventually settling in Rome.

The Order is still based in Rome today, and it still conducts extensive humanitarian work across the planet. *(Source: Ben Bowlin)*

The **Knights of Malta** are the militia of the Pope, and are sworn to total obedience by a blood oath which is taken seriously and to the death. The Pope as the head of the Vatican is also the head of a foreign national power. *(Albert G. Mackey 33rd degree Mason)*

"The painful saga of modern Arab-Muslim history evokes the battles fought in Crusades of the 11th century – when the Knights of Malta began their operations as a Christian militia whose mission it was to defend the land conquered by the Crusaders. These memories return violently to mind with the discovery of links between the so-called security firms in Iraq such as **Blackwater** have historic links with the Order of Malta. You cannot exaggerate it The **Order of Malta** is a hidden government or the most mysterious government in the world." (*Jordanian MP Jamal Muhammad Abidat*)

**Blackwater** is more than just a "private army", much more than just another capitalist war-profiteering business operation. It is an army operating outside all laws, outside and above the U.S. Constitution and yet is controlled by people within and outside our government whose allegiance is primarily to the foreign Vatican state. In other words, **Blackwater** is a religious army serving the Pope in Rome through the **Order of Malta**, which is itself considered under international law, as a sovereign entity with special diplomatic powers and privileges. Like **Blackwater**, the **Order of Malta** is "untouchable" because it is at the heart of the elite aristocracy.

It should be noted that **Blackwater USA** is the brainchild of Erik Prince – a former Navy SEAL and son of Edgar Prince, a wealthy Michigan auto-parts supplier – described as a *"radical right wing Christian mega-millionaire"* who is a strong financial backer of former President George W. Bush, as well as a donor to a host of conservative Christian political causes.

In the 1980's, the Prince family merged with one of the

most venerable conservative families in the U.S.," when Erik's sister Betsy – nine years his senior – married Dick DeVos, whose father Richard, founded the multilevel marketing firm, *Amway*.

The **Knights of Malta** is not merely a "charitable organization". That's just an elaborate front, as should become clear to you later. As the name **Sovereign Military Order of Malta** confirms, it is a military order based on the crusader Knights Hospitaller of Jerusalem and is interwoven with Freemasonry. Most people have never even heard of **SMOM**, much less that it is a part of Freemasonry. But that is the way the aristocratic elite like it.

**Masonic Double-Headed Eagle emblazoned with the Maltese Cross**

This signifies omnipotent royal dominion over both East and West. The orb signifies temporal dominion over the globe of Earth, and the scepter signifies control over the spiritual and religious impulses of humanity. This eagle symbol is used in the Masonic Rite of Memphis and Misraim, under which it reads, "Order Out of Chaos", the Hegelian method of crisis creation. It is found on the seals of many European and Eurasian nation states including that of Russia, indicating direct Vatican control over those countries. It symbolizes the desire of a predatory elite with virtually unlimited resources, to totally dominate the entire world under a **New World Order** global government system using secrecy, manipulation, coercion and terror with the ends justifying the means.

**A Member of
The Knights of Malta**

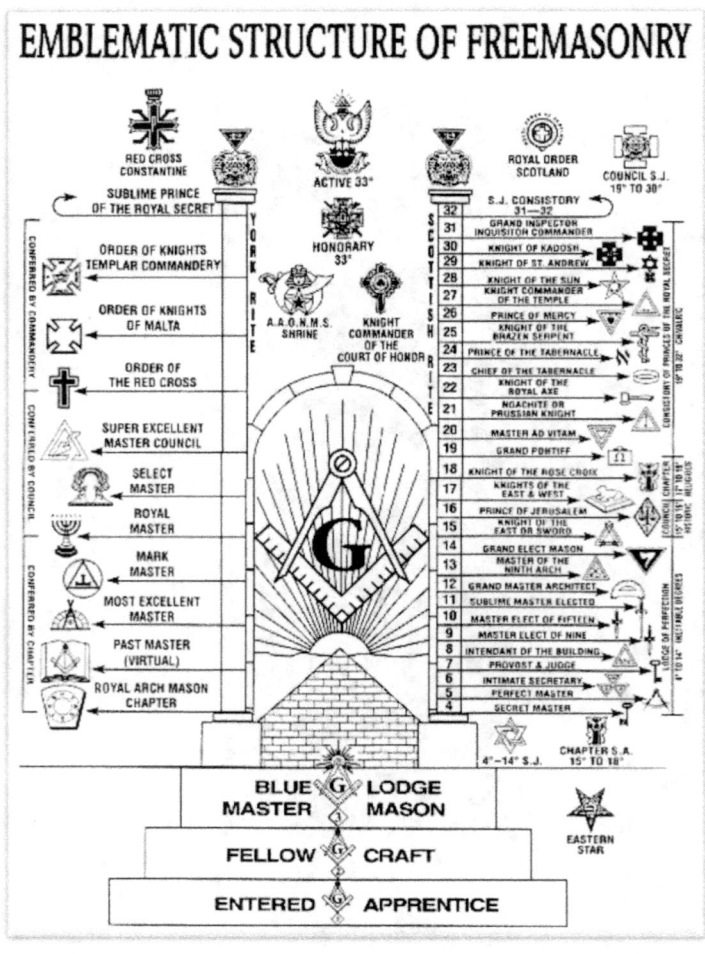

## *The Statue of Liberty and Ishtar*

The *Statue of Liberty* was a Masonic concept conceived from within Freemasonry. The chief promoter and fundraiser for the project was Edward Laboulaye and he collaborated with the sculptor Frederic Bartholdi to develop a statue of Masonic enlightenment. The statue was developed from within the highest doctrines of Freemasonry. This "enlightenment" took its form in various symbols found in the scripture itself.

- The Crown of 7 Spikes:  This symbol was to represent the enlightenment of the Babylonian sun god Shamash/Utu. The idea was that this sun god's occult illumination could be focused by each of the 7 spikes of the crown. Each spike would flash this occult enlightenment to each of the 7 "horas" or large landmasses of the world. In other words, each spike would flash the occult to a continent on planet Earth.
- The Tablets: A common misconception is that the tablets represent the 10 Commandments that

God gave to Moses. This is not true. The tablets are engraved only with the Roman numerals standing for July 4, 1776. The tablets represent a generic notion of the concept of law, not to be confused with the Laws of Moses. Freemasonry gives lip service to Judaism, Christianity, and Islam as law-giving religious but Freemasonry tries to synthesize all religions into one central focus...the idea of "law" in general. Hence the tablets being held by the Statue of Liberty carry that general meaning.

- The Robe: Obviously for reason of monetary purposes, the statue must be made from copper. The use of copper precluded the use of any color schemes of a scarlet and purple robe.
- The Torch: This item was originally designed to be a golden cup filled with the wine of freedom and was actually made. However, before completion and shipping of the entire statue, the New York Port authorities asked if there could be some sort of modification to allow for an eternal flame or light to be designed into the statue so that ships could use her as a night time navigational aid. Bartholdi consented to make modifications to the basic cup design to allow for a natural gas flame to be utilized. The torch we see today is actually the same type of cup design used in ancient times for drinking wine. It featured a handle for the cup at the bottom and the handle looked much like a stick.
- "Mother of Exiles": This is a key term in the poem by Emma Lazarus. In her famous poem about the statue, now etched into the base, Lazarus refers to the woman as *"The Mother of Exiles."* The

poem has forever indelibly linked the statue to immigrants from around the world. The statue is the patron **saint** of immigrants everywhere. Oddly enough, the Babylonian goddess Ishtar was also the patron goddess of immigrants in Babylon because as a goddess of personal freedom, she brought home to immigrants seeking to make a better life for themselves in Babylon. The main claim to fame for Ishtar was pornography – lust fulfillment by sexual relations in exchange for money...holy sexual prostitution. Ishtar worship is the very instance of prostitution in human history and it was deemed "holy!" Now, this may indeed just be an interesting coincidence but remember Revelation 17:5 where the woman called Mystery Babylon is referred to as the *"Mother of Harlots."*

- The Statue of Liberty is the woman described in Revelation 17, 18 and especially 17:4-5, 9 and 18:7 along with Isaiah 47:1-15. We say this because we know that the Statue of Liberty is actually the artist/sculpture's vision of Ishtar, the goddess of Babylon and wife of the false god, Baal. This makes the Statue of Liberty the largest **idol** ever made by human hands.

***The Goddess of ISIS...***has so much love for her children, the souls of creation, that she will allow them to lose themselves in darkness. Her unconditional love is so strong she will allow us to explore ignorance so that we recognize the value of knowledge. And she is always standing with her torch in hand, trying to show us the errors of our ways. She clearly represents evil or impure spiritual forces.

She has no male counterpart. In Natural Law, the principle of Gender refers to the active and passive archetypes of creation. Within the human mind, these are expressed as the passive unconscious mind and the active conscious mind. The ***Principle of Care*** essentially refers to the masculine aspect of desire and action; what we care about is what we take actions to create for ourselves. But if we do not care about truth, wisdom, or goodness, then this will be symbolically depicted as the absence of a male figure next to the feminine archetype of the goddess.

The Statue of Liberty, with her book of wisdom in hand, the crown of light atop her head, and a torch of light held high with her right hand, is the keeper of *lost* wisdom and the guide for *lost* souls.

By all accounts, the alleged terrorist group known as ISIS or ISIL are creations of the Cabal or Illuminati via the CIA.

The seeming goal of this effort is to manipulate the willfully ignorant masses into progressively oppressive and tyrannical social policies so as to become willing slaves for dictatorial elites. And since this program of manipulation can only flourish on the soil of ignorance, the increasing effect over long periods of time is to awaken the masculine nature within each being by the universal mechanism of *pain.*

Pain is a sensation of discomfort which reorients consciousness so as to gain awareness of the thing causing the disease, providing an influx of data to empower the mind with truth, as to change the self and transcend the pain. This is the way the Goddess of ISIS shows us a lack of wisdom which provides an offer to gain knowledge by choosing the truth.

In this way, the ISIS group is acting as a painful experience so that humanity as a whole can muster the courage to seek the truth. This is a type of cosmic initiation, a grand experimentation of consciousness whereby human beings find within themselves the courage to face the truth of their own errors and seek knowledge so as to act wisely in the future.

*For her house leads down to death and her paths to the spirits of the dead. None who go to her return or attain the paths of life.* **Proverbs 2:18-19**

**Will America ever return to**
***We The People*?**

## The Beast,
## False Prophet,
## and Antichrist

The **Beast** as referred to in the **Book of Revelation** behaves as a powerful predatory animal which kills and destroys as it goes about in satisfying its appetite for **power** and **control.** The British Empire is a governmental system that will control an alliance of nations, which will exist a short time before Christ's return. A system of those who administer it are granted absolute authority, power and control over all religious, philosophical, economic and political aspect of the lives of people who come under its control. This religious/political system of government has tremendous economic, industrial, military, and spiritual power at its disposal as it seeks to dominate the entire world.

Three chapters of Revelation show the relationship between the **alliance of nations** (Beast), **the leader of this alliance** (Antichrist and the Beast), and **the Babylonian religious system** (the great Whore led by the False

Prophet).

The **Beast**, **False Prophet**, and the **Antichrist** are not people but a worldwide political system ruled and organized by a supernatural **Satan** and his demonic spirits – those whom I have identified earlier in this book while revealing their secret societies and organizations of world power and authority.

Please note the recorded symbolism in these prophecies pertains to both the physical and spiritual dimensions of existence. The symbolism and references concerning the beasts and horns do not seem to make sense when applied to the physical realm of existence.

The **wild beast** introduced in **Revelation 13:1** represents this worldwide political system I have mentioned – the political part of the Antichrist's system. **And I stood upon the sand of the sea, and saw a beast rise up out of the sea, having seven heads and ten horns, and upon his horns ten crowns, and upon his heads the name of blasphemy.** *It has authority, power, and a throne, which point to its being a political entity.* Both Daniel and John also saw political systems and leaders that they described using the term, **"Beast."** John called it a beast because it comes up out of the sea of "nations" or mixed nationalities. Satan is a counterfeiter, so he has an **"unholy trinity"** that consists of himself **Satan**, the **Antichrist** (the political, religious beast), and the **false prophet** (the religious, political beast). These 'heads' show dominion authority, 'horns' show power, and 'crowns' show kingdom and throne. Blasphemy denies the true God. This beast has the ten horns of power and this is the personification of what Satan does when evil takes over governments and the people who are their leaders.

The seven government heads of the beast of **Revelation 13:1** represent the primary political powers that have dominated through history and have taken the lead in oppressing God's people – Egypt, Assyria, Babylon, Mede-Persia, Greece, Rome, and the British Empire.


Let's take a glance back to the old Roman Empire: It was a vast empire spreading from <u>Britain</u> in the north to south of <u>Egypt</u>, from <u>Spain</u> and <u>North Africa</u> in the west to the borders of Parthia (<u>Iran</u> today) in the east. In the 1$^{st}$ century, when the New Testament was written, the border of the Roman Empire in Europe stopped at the Rhine and Danube Rivers. It never included any significant portion of Germany or Eastern Europe. The center of the Roman Empire was never Gaul (France today). The heart of the Roman Empire in the 1$^{st}$ century were the cities of <u>Rome</u> itself, Alexandria in <u>Egypt</u>, and the <u>Greek cities</u>, with the cities of Antioch, Damascus, and Jerusalem that were inland from the Mediterranean coast; therefore, the Roman Empire was a Mediterranean empire, not a European empire. The Roman Empire also included the province of <u>Turkey</u>.

In some interpretations of the seven nations and/or kings or kingdoms, many are different; therefore, with no absolute degree of certainty can I identify these seven heads and ten horns.


Thus, the wild beast of **Revelation chapter 13** represents a composite political organization. It ascends "out of the sea," that is, from the turbulent masses of mankind that are the source of human governments.


**Revelation 13:2 – And the beast which I saw was like unto a *leopard*, and his feet were as the feet of a *bear*, and his mouth of a *lion*; and the dragon gave him his <u>power</u>, and his <u>seat</u>, and <u>great authority</u>.**

Babylon is symbolized as a lion, Mede-Persia as a bear,

and Greece as the leopard. This Beast includes the people and cultures of the three previous empires, and is an outgrowth of the Roman Empire itself.

It rules over 'every tribe and people and tongue and nation,' so it is greater than a single national government. **Revelation 13:7**

It combines features of the four beasts described in the prophecy of **Daniel 7:2-8**, including the appearance of a leopard, the feet of a bear, a lion's mouth, and ten horns. The beasts in Daniel's prophecy are identified as political kingdoms that rule in succession over empires. **Daniel 7:17, 23 Revelation 13:1, Isaiah 17:12, 13**

The Bible says that the number, or name, of the beast - 666 - is "a man's number." **Revelation 13:17, 18** That expression indicates that the beast of **Revelation chapter 13** is a human entity, not a spirit or demon entity.

Even though nations may agree on few things, they unite in their determination to maintain their authority rather than submit to the rule of God's Kingdom. **(Psalm2:2)** They will also join forces to battle against God's armies commanded by Jesus Christ at Armageddon, but this war will result in the nations being destroyed. **Revelation 16:14, 16; 19:19, 20**

**And I saw one of his heads as it were wounded to death; and his deadly wound was healed: and all the world wondered after the beast. Revelation 13:3**

This is thought to be the decline and disappearance of the old Roman Empire, then the revival of the new Roman Empire. This revival causes amazement throughout the world.

**Revelation 13:4-5 And they worshipped the dragon which gave power unto the beast: and they worshipped the beast, saying, 'Who is like unto the beast? Who is able to make war with him?' And there was given unto him a**

**mouth speaking great things and blasphemies; and power was given unto him to continue forty two months.** John makes it plain that the Beast's power and authority and kingdom are given to him by Satan (verse 2). And John also tells us something revealed to no one else: This is the beginning of the Great Tribulation which Daniel spoke about in when the sacrifice and the oblation ceases, which is called the *Abomination of Desolation*. The power and the authority of the Beast come from Satan himself. Satan has his own false *"trinity"*. <u>Satan acts as the Father</u>, the <u>Antichrist the Son</u>, and the <u>False Prophet as the Spirit</u> who attempts to bring glory to the Antichrist. (verses 11,12).

**Revelation 13:11-12    And I beheld another beast coming up out of the Earth; and he had two horns like a lamb, and he spake as a dragon. And he exerciseth all the power of the first beast before him, and causeth the Earth and them which dwell therein to worship the first beast, whose deadly wound was healed.**

Just as the dragon has already been anti-God and the first Beast is anti-Christ, so the second Beast will be anti-Spirit. He is the False Prophet and will not cause people to worship himself. He will work for the purpose of getting others to worship the Antichrist.

As the Scripture says the Beast will come up out of the Earth (around Palestine), and he perhaps will be an apostate Jew who, during the first 3-1/2 years, will lead Israel to make a covenant with the Antichrist and deceive them by hiding his apostasy until the middle of the Tribulation period, at which time he will reveal his apostate beliefs and practices.

The Lord Jesus Christ is often referred to in the Gospels as the 'Lamb of God', and has taken away the sin of the world. Therefore, the False Prophet coming on the Earth will look like a lamb with two horns. Lambs do ***not*** have horns which are symbols of authority; instead they are meek and mild animals. The Lord Jesus said in the *Sermon on the Mount*, "Watch out for false prophets. They come to you in sheep's clothing, but inwardly they are ferocious wolves." (Matthew 7:15) The False Prophet will come to Israel in sheep's clothing, but God terms him 'a beast'.

Speaking like a dragon, he will develop his power of speech from the devil who is the dragon. This False Prophet will deceive human beings by acting like a lamb while really speaking the words of Satan.

The close relationship between these two world leaders is seen in the fact that the False Prophet will be given power by the Antichrist himself. His whole purpose will be to work toward the complete dominance of the Earth by the Antichrist, including a form of religion satisfactory to the Antichrist.

The False Prophet's main purpose with all this power from the Antichrist and speech from the devil is to lead people to worship the Antichrist. When indwelt by Satan in the middle of the Tribulation, the Antichrist will be so deceived about himself that he will believe he is God and seek the worship of human beings. This form of worship will be circulated by the second beast or False Prophet. He may well be described as the high priest of the Antichrist's religious system during the Tribulation period.

This is the explanation of **The Great Whore of Babylon** and her identity:

**Revelation 17:1**... "I will show unto thee the judgment of the great whore that <u>sitteth upon many waters.</u>" **Revelation 17:15** ..."And he saith unto me, <u>the waters which thou sawest, where the whore sitteth, are peoples, and multitudes</u>." (The Roman Catholic Church is the biggest church in the world with over 1 BILLION members!)

**Revelation 17:2**... "the kings of the Earth have

committed fornication, and the inhabitants of the Earth have been made drunk with the wine of her fornication." (This church has influenced kings throughout the past 2000 years and continues to have 'diplomatic relations' with nations all over the kings of the Earth, which is how the Catholic Church was able to have so many Christians killed during the dark ages and inquisitions.)

**Revelation 17:4** ..."And the woman was arrayed in purple and scarlet color, and decked with gold and precious stones and pearls, having a golden cup in her hand full of abominations and filthiness of her fornication." (The main colors of this church are Purple and Scarlet which the Bishops and Cardinals wear. The Vatican is decked out with gold and precious stones. Some of the coins the Vatican has had produced have images of a woman with a golden cup in her hand on them, blatantly boasting of who she is! The cup full of abominations is also a symbol that the sins of this church are so great that it is now a fallen, apostate church that can never be the church of Christ Jesus. The sins of the Roman Catholic Church are immense, with its idolatry, murder, and child abuse that she has committed throughout her history and continues to commit.)

**Revelation 17:5**..."And upon her forehead was a name written, Mystery, Babylon the Great, the Mother of Harlots and Abominations of the Earth." (So the whore of Babylon is shrouded in mystery and the only church we know that to be is the Roman Catholic Church with their secrets and including what really goes on behind closed doors at the Vatican; not to mention the mysterious behavior with the Papacy. **Mother of Harlots**? – the Protestant churches came out of the Roman Catholic Church. There is no other church that has **"harlot daughters"** like the Papal Church of Rome does. And she is even regarded as the *"Mother"* church. Babylon from the Old Testament is the original mother of abominations, but the Roman Catholic Church is the spiritual mother of abominations that took on many of the Pagan customs of original Babylon.)

**Revelation 17:6**…"And I saw the woman <u>drunken with the blood of the saints</u>; and with the blood of the martyrs of Jesus." (This church is not only guilty of killing a few Christians but she is guilty of killing **many, many** of God's people. The Roman Catholic Church has caused TENS of MILLIONS of Christians to be persecuted and brutally murdered? This woman is the Roman Catholic Church for sure!)

**Revelation 17:18**…"And the woman which thou sawest is that great city, which reigneth over the kings of the Earth." (We know Babylon the Great is a church. Bringing the church and the city together we know there is a city that "reigns" over the nations of the world. That city which has diplomatic relations with virtually all the world's nations is the *Vatican City*! The papacy is so influential and powerful that nearly every major country consults her before making major policy moves.)

**Revelation 17:6**…"and <u>when I saw her, I wondered with great admiration</u>." (The Roman Catholic Church with all her splendor. Millions of people flock to the Vatican every year as they marvel in admiration of her **"majesty"**.)

**Revelation 17:3**…"and I saw a woman sit upon a scarlet colored beast, full of names of blasphemy, having seven heads and ten horns." (This beast is the same as the 'red dragon' in Revelation chapter 12. That dragon is Satan, 'that old serpent called the devil.' The beast in Revelation 13 also has seven heads and ten horns. However, Revelation 17 tells us those ten horns represent kings/kingdoms. So, this dragon not only represents Satan, but also has a civil power.)

The **"whore"** riding and controlling the beast is the city of Rome, represented today by the *Club of Rome*, the *Jesuits*, and *Vatican City*, all working together in their intricate recital – the secret societies of which I have described. This established system of evil controllers is very proud of what they intend to accomplish; however, in the end they are really begging for God's judgment to come down on their heads. Taking counsel against the Lord and his anointed will surely be their horrendous demise.

**Revelation 12:4**..."and the dragon stood before the woman which was ready to be delivered, <u>for to devour her child as soon as it was born</u>." (So the dragon waited for this child to be born to kill him. Who was the child? Revelation 12:5 tells us that he was "caught up to God and His throne." There is only one *male* child which ended up going to heaven and more specifically to God's own throne, and that was Jesus Christ. So this child whom Satan wanted to devour as soon as He was born was Jesus. And who did Satan use to try and kill Jesus when He was born? The king of ROME. So this 'red dragon' also represents Rome. And, this woman gets her 'seat' and 'authority' from Rome. And the Roman Catholic Church gets her seat and authority from Rome!)

No other church, religion, kingdom or institution matches the Roman Catholic Church like the Papal Church of Rome does. God is calling His people out of Babylon and the other fallen churches of the world who are Babylon's daughters!

## *World Trade Center Twin Towers – 9/11*

It was revealed that nuclear devises used September 11, 2001 in the destruction of the *World Trade Center* Twin *Towers* in New York City were a modified version of the W-54 nuclear artillery shells. These had been covertly provided to the Israelis between 1988 and 1998 from US surplus stockpiles illegally exported during the Bush/Clinton era. The Department of Energy had sent these W-54 shells to a storage dump in Amarillo, Texas to later be converted into fuel.

Chemical analysis was done by DOE Sandi who was able to identify the chemical/radiation footprint of the plutonium-based warheads founded on samples taken after 9/11 of the fallout at ground zero.

This was the 9/11 blackmail for Bush I and 2 because of their illegal transfer of surplus US nuclear weapons to the Israelis and the continued cover-up, along with the stolen gold and stock fraud that was happening on Wall Street.

Only a 2 kiloton device was needed to drop the WTC

twin towers, which produced a fireball of approximately 150-200 in diameter at over 4000 degrees in Centigrade, large enough to melt the I-beams of the central core of the building and drop them in place. The underground detonation intended to vaporize 150-300 feet of 6 inch thick steel I-beams that constituted the central core of both towers, which created a fire ball event as broadcasted on television for everyone to view.

Fallout was minimal and located to around zero range only. Radiation would drop to acceptable levels within 72 hours after the blast. Most fallout was trapped in the cement dust thus causing all of the recent cancer deaths reported in New York City amongst the first responders. The **U.S. government** coordinated conspiracy to commit high treason, mass murder, grand theft and premeditated acts of state-sponsored terrorism:

- Twin towers were destroyed by nuclear weapons.
- Planned destruction of towers in NYC partially done as *nuclear blackmail*, and to also *stop investigation of $200 trillion theft and 350 nuclear warheads.*
- Nuclear "pits", the center of warheads were sent by Department of Energy to the Pantex Plant in Amarillo, Texas to convert into fuel.
- Between 1988 and 1994, the Israelis began cherry-picking to re-build the Israeli nuclear arsenal after the Dimona nuclear reactor operation had crashed.
- When Israelis were no longer able to produce nuclear weapons, they found a way to take them off the shelf in the USA. The only way they could achieve that was with the help of a <u>high level mole</u> within the Department of Energy who could tell them which ones to take. *(This is likely one of the biggest national secrets ever!)* This conspiracy group controls members of Congress by running

gambling money through Las Vegas and Macau, operating prostitution and [rent boys] groups across the USA and through Washington, DC. **The group controls a massive blackmail organization out of Cuba.**

- Osama Bin Laden was a phantom enemy created to mask the real enemy, and only enemy, the **Director of Homeland Security**. It turned out to be a horrible mistake that the USA hand-fed weapons into Al-Nusra ISIL, after code naming them *Al Qaeda*; so they burned up the name *Al Qaeda.*

- The real Osama Bin Laden, and head of *Al Qaeda*, was the **Director of Homeland Security**, and ran *Al Qaeda* with the help of a <u>U.S. Attorney</u>, head of wealthy Canadian distilling family, alleged Mayor of NYC, a NYC police commissioner – all involved in planning 9/11 according to documents. Also the President of South Africa, and the Prime Minister of Israel, and a prominent White House Counter-Terrorism official were secretly involved.

- Names NOT listed in the document are Donald Rumsfeld, John Ashcroft, Dick Cheney, and George W. Bush. There are classification levels in that particular document that are not legal to list according to Gordon Duff who wrote this article. **This investigation into theft of nuclear weapons is being handled by a federal grand jury in Houston, Texas that is still seated**. There are a number of people currently in witness protection. There are numerous — "piles" — of witness statements involving people who had driven nuclear weapons in refrigeration trucks full of cow carcasses. The nuclear weapons were in boxes on the floor under the carcasses. Nuclear weapons were then sorted inside a refrigeration facility and transferred to fertilizer plants, ultimately moved through the Port of Houston. The truck drivers and people who butchered and cut up the cows who have made incriminating statements have been in witness protection for many years.

- On 9/11 the destroyed Pentagon offices contained a small G2 Unit, which was a highly classified Criminal Investigation Service. The part of the Pentagon that was hit was the site of the Able Danger offices. They were investigating missing nuclear weapons and 35 out of 50 key investigators from the group, *Able Danger,* were killed in that attack. The area where the missile struck was where they had been called into the office for an "emergency general staff meeting" that was running late.

- The people they were protecting in southern Manhattan from a nuclear attack on 9/11 – CEO's of key firms working in the World Trade Center – were invited to a private golf outing, but in reality were kept secure at Offutt Air Force Base in Nebraska. ***Golf outing was sponsored by Warren Buffet.***

- There is a list of an alleged 125 casualties at the Pentagon, exclusive of the 'plane crash' victims, whereas 36 of them were financial analysts, accountants, and budget experts. It was suggested that Donald Rumsfeld, Secretary of Defense, had used the occasion to mention **$2.3 trillion was missing from the budget**, in order to get them all together in the West Block offices of the Pentagon, with their documents and records, to take them out.

- The 9/11 tragedy is one facet of their 'house

cleaning', blackmail, and a massive case of insurance fraud. *9/11 was big – a very big PAYDAY killing off as many people as possible!*

- Witnesses and many others fear for their lives. Many people in the USA are under gag orders from Federal Judges who have all the information about 9/11 bought, and killed all the family's enemies.

- They did that and made a *$7 billion payday*, and after that they put in place different organizations. They took a primary 9/11 plotter and put him in charge of the Department of Homeland Security where all investigations could be quashed immediately. All of the criminal cases tied to 9/11 went to a US Attorney who was involved in 9/11 planning. The most powerful lobbying groups in Washington and 'think tanks' were all involved in planning 9/11.

- Of course, there were pay-offs to silence the people. What is a life worth? **$20 million?** They went through Congress, department after department, through the FBI, Department of Justice, and gave these people **$20 million.** Accounting was done in the Caribbean and handled through the Cayman Islands. All these people now, hundreds of them who know everything about the terror of 9/11, are sitting there with **$20 million**, and Obama just cut them off from their cash.

- They don't just hand you the money; they launder the money for you because they have banks, and they control the IRS, and they control the Treasury Department. They are the ones who make sure you never get audited, that nobody looks through your accounts for the money, that none of it is ever seen. You can take money in and out of the country, and you can keep it. However, if anything ever goes wrong, <u>they can always get you</u>. To come forward and testify means nothing because <u>you will never live</u> to see a judge; a police officer can always pull you over and shoot you! Or you can die like Mike Connell who refused to obey Karl Rove and made him angry, so his plane hit a sand bank. Or you'll have a mysterious heart attack, or a strange case of systematically induced cancer. Failed attempt was made on <u>Gordon Duff</u>'s life; however, he has felt it necessary to provide you, the reader, with all of this information.

Illegal distribution of US nuclear material to foreign allies was not limited to just Israel. Virtually all NATO allies were in on this scam too. Dick Cheney was the bad guy on this one. Bush 2/Cheney traded nuclear pits to foreign countries as IOU's in order to get what they wanted.

Tom Countryman, a well-known Israeli operative, is *curiously* now in charge of N.N.P. at the State Department under Obama and has been the Assistant Secretary of State for International Security and Nonproliferation since September 27, 2011. The Net National Product is the monetary value of finished goods and services produced by a country's citizens, whether overseas or resident, in the time period being measured. Countryman was put in his position by Rahm Emanuel who was White House chief of staff to Obama, and then elected Mayor of Chicago in 2011.

## *The Iran Nuclear Deal*

The Iran nuclear deal agreement was reached in 2015 between the Islamic Republic of Iran and a group of world powers (the permanent members of the United Nations Security Council – the **P5+1**) and the European Union.

The **P5+1** refers to the Council's five permanent members; namely China, France, Russia, the United Kingdom, and the United States; plus Germany. The **P5+1** is often referred to as the **E3+3** by European countries. It is a group of six world powers which, in 2006, joined together in diplomatic efforts with Iran with regard to *its nuclear program.*

In June 2006, China, Russia, and the U.S. joined the three *EU-3 countries*, which had been negotiating with Iran since 2003, to offer another proposal for comprehensive negotiations with Iran. Agreement discussions throughout the different countries of the **P5+1** continued until 2015.

Negotiations for a framework deal over the nuclear program of Iran took place between the foreign ministers of the countries at a series of meetings held from March 26 to April 2, 2015 in Lausanne, Switzerland. The **Joint Comprehensive Plan of Action**, otherwise known as the **Iran Nuclear Deal**, was finally reached in Vienna on July 14, 2015 between Iran, the **P5+1** and the **European Union** with the agreed amount of **$150 billion** to be paid by the United States and other allies.

Part of the severe sanctions that were imposed on Iran included restrictions on banking. Iran had sold, and delivered, large quantities of oil to several countries, including China, India, Japan, and South Korea. But they were not able to pay for the oil, so the money was kept in banks in those countries.

As part of the *Joint Comprehensive Plan of Action* *neg*otiated between Iran and the **P5+1**, and unanimously approved by the UN Security Council, the banking restrictions were lifted. Iran was then able to receive its own money, that had been withheld.

The agreement was also reached that Iran would redesign, convert, and reduce its nuclear facilities and accept the Additional Protocol (with provisional application) in order to lift the nuclear-related economical sanctions, freeing up tens of billions of dollars in oil revenue and frozen assets. In addition to the joint statement, the U.S. and Iran issued fact sheets of their own.

In a speech on the Saturday following July 22nd, Iran's Supreme Leader Ayatollah Ali Khamenei stated, *"Our policy will not change with regards to the arrogant U.S. government."* Iran will be required to provide the International Atomic Energy Agency access to all of its declared facilities so that the agency can be sure as to the peaceful nature of the nuclear program.

President Barack Obama said a "historic understanding" had been reached with Iran, and pointed out that the deal with Iran is a good deal if it can meet core objectives of the

United States.

150 Democratic Congress members signaled that they support reaching a deal, enough to sustain a Presidential Veto. Majority of Congress including all Republicans and some Democrats opposed the deal. *(Source: Wikipedia)*

## The Four Hundred Million Dollar Debt

During Jimmy Carter's presidency in November 1979, a group loyal to the revolutionary regime took 52 Americans hostage at the U.S. Embassy in Tehran. They were held for 444 days in Iran. In response, the U.S. severed diplomatic relations with Iran and froze their assets in America and halted a delivery of fighter jets for which they had already paid **$400 million.** The U.S. would have normally returned the money since they did not deliver the planes; however, they had already frozen Iran's assets as punishment for the hostage-taking.

Two years later – 1981 – the hostage crisis was resolved at a  conference in Algiers when President Ronald Reagan was being inaugurated. However, the legal status of Iran's **$400 million** had not been settled. Instead, an international court based in the Hogue was set up to deal with legal claims the Iran and U.S. governments might have against each other.

The court, known as the Iran-United States Claims Tribunal, functioned as an essential arbitration for either negotiations out of court or the case before a panel of three US-appointed judges, three Iranian-appointed judges, and three neutral judges. They would hear the case and the panel would determine a binding ruling.

Thirty-five years passed and the extremely slow process continued into President Obama's second term in office. The tribunal had yet to come to a ruling on the matter of Iran's **$400 million.**

The U.S. government then concluded it was going to lose the case as Iran was seeking **$10 billion** with high interest payments. So, the Obama administration decided to settle out of court while opening negotiations with Iran on the terms of the settlement. They did this at the same time of negotiation of the nuclear deal and the return of four U.S. citizens who had been detained by Iran more recently. Those working on the nuclear deal and the prisoner release were a different team from the ones working on the court case concerning the weapons money ($400 million).

The countries finally settled on a deal by January 2016 whereby the U.S. would pay Iran **$1.7 billion**, which amounted to **$1,300,000,000** <u>interest</u> on top of the originally frozen assets which accounted for inflation. The **$400 million** payment from the *Judgment Fund* was the first installment paid on January 17th with the interest payment that followed on January 19th and also on February 5th via Swiss banks. Installments were made because U.S. law prevents the U.S. government from giving Iran dollars, so the government had to gather foreign currency, which was difficult and required **the installment plan.**

The so-called *Judgment Fund* is taxpayer money Congress has permanently approved in the event it's needed, allowing the president to bypass direct congressional approval to make a settlement.

Thirty-five years of a mind-numbing, international

litigation was totally unrelated to the nuclear and prisoner deal. The payment was not for "ransom" as many had publicly suggested, even though the U.S. withheld payment of **$1.7 billion** in secret cash until Iran released four U.S. prisoners. *(Source: Daily Mail)*

## *Hillary Diane Rodham Clinton*

Hillary Diane Rodham Clinton was born October 26, 1947 in Chicago, Illinois. She was raised in Park Ridge, a suburb located 15 miles northwest of downtown Chicago. Her parents were Hugh E. Rodham, businessman, and Dorothy Emma Howell Rodham. She is of Welsh, English, French and French Canadian ancestry. Hillary grew up with two younger brothers, Hugh and Tony.

She studied at Maine East High School and Maine South High School. She finished high school in 1965, and enrolled at Wellesley College in Massachusetts. In 1969, Rodham entered Yale Law School. Hillary received a Juris Doctor degree from Yale in 1973. Then, she began a year of post-graduate study on children and medicine at the Yale Child Study Center.

Hillary Rodham married Bill Clinton on October 11, 1975 in a Methodist ceremony in their living room in a 980-square foot home in the Hillcrest neighborhood of Little Rock, where they resided until 1979.

In 1979, Hillary became the first woman partner at Rose

Law Firm through the support and influence of two partners, Vince Foster and Webster Hubbell. When her husband, Bill Clinton, became the governor of Arkansas, as First Lady, she led a task force and served on several corporate boards. She often stated, "Human rights are women's rights and women's rights are human rights," thus being in support of pro-choice and the abortion of babies and embryo's.

Her marriage endured the Monica Lewinsky scandal of 1998, and her role as first lady drew a polarized response from the public while in the White House.

In 2000, Hillary was elected as the first female senator from New York, the only first lady every to have sought elective office. Following the September 11 attacks, she voted to approve the war in Afghanistan. She also voted for the Iraq Resolution, which she later regretted. She was re-elected to the Senate in 2006. Running for president in 2008, she won far more delegates than any previous female candidate, but lost the Democratic nomination to Illinois Senator Barack Obama.

Hillary served as Secretary of State under the Obama administration from 2009-2013. Leaving office after Obama's first term, she wrote her fifth book and undertook speaking engagements before announcing her second presidential run in the 2016 election. Receiving the most votes and primary delegates in the 2016 Democratic primaries, she formally accepted her party's nomination for President of the United States on July 28, 2016, with vice presidential running mate, **Senator Tim Kaine** who is a long-time Jesuit adjutor. Hillary became the first female candidate to be nominated for president by a major U.S. political party. As part of her platform, she has emphasized raising incomes, improvements to the Affordable Care Act and reform of campaign finance and Wall Street. She favors allowing pathways to citizenship for undocumented immigrants, expanding and protecting LGBT and women's rights, and instituting family support through paid parental leave and universal preschool.

Hillary Clinton's failing health has been speculated about for years; however, now that she is on the campaign trail, many are starting to ask more serious questions.

Dr. Drew Pinsky recently reported: "She's had a clot in her leg – these are serious clots that lead to something called pulmonary embolism, which can also cause sudden death. So, she has an underlying recurrent blood clot in her leg, a clot in her transverse sinus...why is she clotting?" he asked.

He continued, "We wonder why Hillary is taking an *"anticoagulant"*, which is a blood thinner called Coumadin for the clots she had years ago when there is supposedly no underlying condition currently? Usually it isn't used for more than two months, which is a clear sign that something else is wrong.

She has to be monitored closely, as the drug insures she can bleed under the skin easily by bumping into things. An auto accident could cause bleeding to death since the blood clots would not properly form."

Dr. Drew also noted: "And then why would you leave her on the oldest and sort of most treacherous anticoagulant? If you're going to leave somebody on an anticoagulant, why the oldest, old fashion anticoagulant...Wouldn't you think somebody who's a candidate for president (would) have one of the newer anticoagulants that are safer?"

At Hillary's age of 68, a clot could lead to pulmonary embolism (clot traveling to the lungs)...which damages the lungs or other organs. It could also cause a stroke and kill her.

Her closest advisor and body-woman, Huma Abedin, has

admitted on State Department emails that Hillary is sick and "often confused". And Matt Drudge has noted Hillary's possible use of a "walker" during magazine photo shoots.

Dr. Drew Pinsky's television show has been cancelled as of this date. *(Source: The Political Insider)*

**Dr. Ben Carson,** top neurosurgeon and former presidential candidate, recently shared his thoughts with Fox News' Sean Hannity: "It's critical for Hillary Clinton to release her full medical history given intensifying questions over her health as a presidential candidate."

Noting that Hillary's age is a reason to be on the lookout for any worsening medical conditions, Carson said that it was "critical" for Clinton to undergo a medical examination given the important position she may be about to take.

He continued as he said, "That information should be something we have access to because it's very important in terms of making that decision – also recognize that the presidency is not a nine to five job – it is extraordinarily grueling and you need to have everything going for you." He also added that a mental examination should also be required of Hillary, and further stated, "These are the kind of things that should be open to the public in making such a critical decision...there's no way we should even consider doing it without having a look at those records."

Dr. Marc Siegel joined the conversation in stating that Hillary's fall in 2012 could have caused brain damage that leads to long term problems with memory, thinking, dizziness, and walking. He added that the videos which show Hillary having "brain freeze" where she can't remember words or the last thing she said was worthy of "more investigation."

Respondents to a recent poll have wanted to see Hillary release her medical history. However, leftist media outlets have framed questions over Hillary's health as a "conspiracy theory" and refute any allegations as to her not being physically and mentally capable to be our Commander in Chief.

The media is owned and controlled by a great and most powerful hierarchy in our world – the Illuminati and the Jesuit Order.

Very few people understand the hidden world power structure which I have tried to previously explain. As the **Chosen People**, there's no question that the Jews were 'chosen' to run Hollywood (they're great comedians), the banking and investment industry (they were the first to charge interest), the medical and legal professions (they have golden hands and silver tongues), as well as a number of other important spheres of life.

However, the leaders in each of these major arenas, which are used to control Western societies everywhere, suffer from extremely high visibility. Exposure is the first thing that real power-brokers and controllers strive hard to avoid. Those who really control the Earthly realm operate in complete secrecy. They always have and they always will since it is secrecy that is the very basis of their power and influence.

No one knows this face of life on Earth better than the Society of Jesus – the Jesuits. Everyone knows exactly who the Jesuit General is at any given point in time since he's totally out there and is completely exposed – just another pawn on the massive global geopolitical chessboard. Yes, he does exercise great power in the administration of the *World Shadow Government*, but, at the end of the day, every military arm is just that, a disposable arm that does a lot of dirty work.

<u>The Trinity of Globalist Control</u>:
- Vatican City - Rome, Italy     **Religion**
- City of London, England     **Finance**
- Washington, D.C., USA     **Military**

Just as the U.S. is the military arm of the New World Order (NWO) headquartered in Washington, D.C. and the United Kingdom is the financial arm of the NWO based in the Financial District in the City of London, the Black Nobility of Jesuit Freemasonry controls the Vatican which has forever functioned as the religious arm. Only with this correct knowledge can the many levels of power and influence which exist above these three power centers be properly understood.

**Hillary Rodham Clinton**

*Can a corrupt throne be allied with you – one that brings on misery by its decrees? They band together against the righteous and condemn the innocent to death.*
**Psalm 94:20-21**

## *How does Vice-Presidential candidate Tim Kaine fit in?*

Timothy Michael "Tim" Kaine was born February 26, 1958 in Saint Paul, Minnesota, and grew up in Overland Park, Kansas. He graduated from the University of Missouri, and earned a law degree from Harvard Law School before entering private practice.

Kaine was mayor of Richmond, Virginia from 1998-2001 and Lieutenant Governor of Virginia from 2002-2005.

In 2005 he ran for governor of Virginia and won. His campaign had turned sharply negative when his opponent, Jerry W. Kilgore, claimed in his ads that Kaine believed "Hitler" doesn't qualify for the death penalty. The ads also attacked Kaine for his service ten years earlier as a court-appointed attorney for a death-row inmate.

In 2012 Kaine was elected to the Senate, and this year he has become nominee for the Democratic Vice-President to Presidential candidate Hillary Clinton.

Tim Kaine operates on the very same level as the Jesuit-controlled Joe Biden. The Biden family is a Georgetown-educated one. As I will explain in a following article on Bill Clinton, Georgetown University is the Jesuit training ground that he attended and it is used to groom all of America's diplomats and statesmen at that highly regarded School of International Affairs. Whoever attends, and then enters public life at a high level, is most assuredly a Jesuit operative for the rest of their political career.

Biden, unknown to but a few, is Obama's real handler. And of course, Valerie Jarrett functions as his *brain*. Many of the VP's throughout recent U.S. history have been chosen as point-men in the White House who really work for the NWO ruling elites. These globalists-at-heart have only one mission in mind. This is why Biden was chosen to act as the cheerleader in charge of taking away America's guns. While he often appears to be a total buffoon, this is but an **act** to deflect any serious inquiry about the actual power that he carries in the Oval Office.

Tim Kaine was chosen because of his strong Jesuit education and pedigree. A Jesuit-trained Irish Catholic of his stature is just what is needed by the NWO faction should a President Hillary Clinton become a reality. Were she to become POTUS, she would either be impeached (resulting in Kaine becoming POTUS), incapacitated by her many physical and mental deficits (resulting in Kaine becoming POTUS), or die by Jesuit intrigue or natural death (resulting in Kaine becoming POTUS). Even if she finishes out her term, she still holds an amount of power to which Jesuits control her to have (as long as she is obedient to them).

There is much more to the part that Tim Kaine will play in a Clinton Administration which is quite similar to Joe Biden. Both of these men were chosen because of their allegiance to the agenda of gross liberalization of America. It was Biden who kept the *Manchurian Candidate* Obama on track with this evil scheme to irreparably tear apart the social fabric of the American Republic. While Obama was indoctrinated to perform this role, it is Biden who keeps the frequent golfer in line as the nation crashes and burns.

*Illuminati-puppet*, Tim Kaine, is enthusiastically for total gun control, unlimited illegal immigration, open borders, gay marriage, unobstructed abortion, LGBT normalization, among many other unlawful and immoral positions. He will also then be used to advance this same ultra-liberal agenda that Obama began almost eight disastrous years ago. About this there can be no doubt which is why "good" Catholics are chosen in the first place. Their images are utilized to demonstrate respectability on what is truly a warped evil agenda and demonic enterprise. That overarching and global enterprise is known as the **New World Order.** *(Source: NBC/beforeitsnews.com)*

**Tim Kaine**

*Whether you turn to the right or to the left, your ears will hear a voice behind you, saying, "This is the way; walk in it."* **Isaiah 30:21**

## Who is Huma Mahmood Abedin in relationship to Hillary Clinton?

Born in 1976 in Kalamazoo, Michigan, **Huma Mahmood Abedin** is the daughter of Syed Abedin (1928-1993), Indian-born scholar who in the early 1970's was affiliated with Muslim Students Association at Western Michigan University. Huma's mother, Saleha Mahmood Abedin, is a sociologist known for her strong advocacy of Sharia Law. A member of the Muslim Sisterhood (i.e., the Muslim Brotherhood's division for women), Saleha is also a board member of the International Islamic Council for Dawa and Relief. This pro-Hamas entity is part of the Union of Good, which the U.S. government has formally designated as an international terrorist organization led by the **Muslim Brotherhood.**

When Huma was two, the Abedin family relocated from Michigan to Jeddah, Saudi Arabia. At age 18, Huma Abedin returned to the U.S. to attend George Washington University. In 1996, the quiet young lady began working as an intern in the Bill Clinton White House where she was assigned to then-First Lady Hillary Rodham Clinton. (At the very same time, another young lady, Monica Lewinsky became intern for President Bill Clinton). Abedin was eventually hired as an aide to Mrs. Clinton and has worked for her ever since, through Clinton's successful Senate runs (in 2000 and 2006) and her failed presidential bid in 2008.

From 1997 until sometime before early 1999, Abedin, while still interning at the White House, was an executive board member of George Washington University's (GWU) Muslim Students Association (MSA), heading the organization's "Social Committee."

It is noteworthy that in 2001-02, soon after Abedin left that executive board, the chaplain and "spiritual guide" of GWU's MSA was Anwar Al-Awlaki, the A operative who ministered to some of the men who were among the 9/11 hijackers. Another chaplain at GWU's MSA (from at least October 1999 through April 2002) was Mohamed Omeish, who headed the International Islamic Relief Organization, which has been tied to the funding of Al Qaeda. Omeish's brother, Esam, headed the Muslim American Society, the Muslim Brotherhood's quasi-official branch in the United States. Both brothers were closely associated with Abdurrahman Alamoudi who was later incarcerated on terrorism charges.

From 1996-2008, Abedin was employed by the Institute of Muslim Minority Affairs (IMMA) as the assistant editor of the Journal of Muslim Minority Affairs (JMMA). At least the first seven of those years overlapped with the Al Qaeda-affiliated Abdullah Omar Naseef's active presence at IMMA. Abedin's last six years at the Institute (2002-2008) were spent as a JMMA editorial board member when Naseef and Abedin served together on that board.

Throughout her years with IMMA, Abedin remained a close aide to Hillary Clinton. During Mrs. Clinton's 2008 presidential primary campaign, a New York Observer profile of Abedin described her as "a trusted advisor to Mrs. Clinton, especially on issues pertaining to the Middle East, according to a number of Clinton associates. And at meetings on the region, Ms. Abedin's perspective is always sought out."

When Mrs. Clinton was appointed as President Barack Obama's Secretary of State in 2009, Abedin became her Deputy Chief of Staff.

Apart from their working relationship, Abedin and Mrs. Clinton have also developed a close personal bond over their years together. In 2011, Secretary Clinton paid a friendly visit to Abedin's mother, Saleha, in Saudi Arabia. On that occasion, Mrs. Clinton publicly described her aide's position as "very important and sensitive."

On July 10, 2010, Huma Abedin, a practicing Muslim, married then-congressman Anthony Weiner (aka Carlos Danger) in a ceremony officiated by former president Bill Clinton. A number of analysts have noted it extremely rare for Islamic women, particularly those whose families have ties to the Muslim Brotherhood, to marry non-Muslims like Weiner who is Jewish. Indeed, Dr. Anwar Shoeb, the highest-ranking faculty authority at the prestigious College of Sharia and Islamic Studies in Kuwait, formally declared that Abedin's marriage to Weiner was "null and void" under the dictates of Sharia Law which explicitly forbids matrimony between a Muslim woman and an "infidel". In fact, Shoeb classified the Abedin-Weiner union as a form of "adultery."

Abedin went on maternity leave after giving birth to a baby boy in early December 2011. When she returned to work in June 2012, the State Department granted her an arrangement that allowed her to earn outside income as a private consultant, even as she remained a top advisor in the Department. This arrangement was made possible when Mrs. Clinton personally signed off on documents dated March 23, 2012 that changed Abedin's title from "Deputy Chief of Staff" to "Special Government Employee." Abedin's outside clients included the U.S. State Department, Hillary Clinton, the Clinton Foundation, and Teneo (a New York-based global advisory firm co-founded by Doug Band, former counselor for Bill Clinton).

Abedin did not disclose on her financial report either the special employment arrangement or the $135,000 she earned from it, in violation of a law mandating that public officials reveal significant sources of income. In fact, her title change did not become public knowledge until May 2013. Good-government groups warned of the potential conflict-of-interest inherent in an arrangement where a government employee maintains private clients.

Documents obtained by Judicial Watch in a Freedom Of Information Act (FOIA) lawsuit showed that both before and after Mrs. Clinton signed off on the special employment deal for Abedin in March 2012, Abedin repeatedly, for months on end, dodged State Department requests that she disclose financial and employment information about her husband, Anthony Weiner, who had left Congress amid personal scandal in June 2011.

In June 2012, five lawmakers sent letters to the Departments of Homeland Security, Justice, and State asking they investigate whether the Muslim Brotherhood was gaining undue influence over U.S. government officials. One letter, noting that Huma Abedin's position with Hillary Clinton "affords her routine access to the secretary [of state] and to policymaking," expressed concern over the fact that Abedin "has three family members; her late father, mother and her brother, connected to Muslim Brotherhood operatives and/or organizations."

On February 1, 2013, Hillary Clinton's final day as Secretary of State, Abedin resigned her post as Mrs. Clinton's Deputy Chief of Staff, yet she would continue to serve as a "very close aide" to Clinton.

In early March 2015, it was reported that throughout her entire four-year tenure as Secretary of State (SOS), Hillary Clinton had never acquired or used a government email account, and instead had transmitted -- in violation of government regulations -- all of her official government correspondences via a personal email account that was housed on a private server. In addition, Abedin and Mrs. Clinton's chief of staff, Cheryl Mills, also had email addresses on the secret server while employed at the State Department.

After Hillary Clinton announced in the spring of 2015 that she was running for president (2016), Abedin was named Vice-chair of the Clinton campaign. Huma Abedin turned 40 recently and Hillary Clinton is 69.

Huma Abedin's brother, Hassan Abedin, still has ties to the Muslim Brotherhood.

Beautiful feminine Muslim Huma Abedin who dresses in the latest of fashions has a very close relationship with Hillary Clinton who maintains her less feminine style of pantsuits and "heavy Chinese coats". They have shared this friendship for more than two decades along with their similar strengths and beliefs. Both have husbands who have cheated. Both have a child each.... Huma Abedin testified last year for eight hours about the "personal" and "classified" e-mails.

Recently Huma Abedin and husband, Anthony Weiner, have separated, and she has reported this is the final straw for him! Undoubtedly, Hillary Clinton has given Huma her blessings for doing as instructed.

Bill Clinton had performed their ceremony while both he and Hillary felt it would make for a great appearance if they were married while removing any allegations of an *"intimate relationship."*

**Hillary R. Clinton and her body-woman,
Huma Mahmood Abedin**

*Blessed is the nation whose God is the Lord, the people He chose for His inheritance.* **Psalm 33:12**

The Bible clearly teaches that those who go to hell do so because they *reject the truth*. Unbelievers will be deceived by an Antichrist and perish because they did not receive the love of the truth so as to be saved.

*Who is the liar? It is the man who denies that Jesus is the Christ. Such a man is the antichrist. He denies the Father and the Son.* **1 John 2:22**

The terrifying reality is that God will seal the fate of those who hate the gospel by sending upon them a deluding influence so that they will believe what is false. The Antichrist will deceive people with satanically empowered false miracles, signs, and wonders, his deception only will succeed because it fits into God's sovereign purpose. He will sentence unbelievers to accept evil as if it were good and lies as if they were the truth. Those who continually choose falsehood will be intricately caught up in it. They will be abandoned by God to the consequences of their choice to reject the gospel.

*The evil deeds of a wicked man ensnare him; the cords of his sin hold him fast.* **Proverbs 5:22**

## *William Jefferson Blythe III*

William Jefferson Blythe, III was born in Hope, Arkansas. His biological father, William Jefferson Blythe, Jr. died in a car accident three months before Bill Clinton was born. His mother, Virginia Clinton Kelley was a Nurse anesthetist. He took the last name Clinton because it was his stepfather, Roger Clinton, Sr.'s name. Clinton grew up in Hot Springs, Arkansas. In high school, Clinton played the saxophone. He went to college at Georgetown University where he was Jesuit-trained and close to the Jesuit faculty. He was groomed to be a powerful political leader. During his college years, Clinton worked under several politicians. He later went to Oxford University and Yale Law School. Clinton did not fight in the Vietnam War because he was in the ROTC for a short time. Hillary and Bill Clinton met in the Yale Law School Library in the early 1970's while they were classmates. The Clinton's only child is daughter Chelsea Clinton Mezvinsky, born on February 27, 1980.

Clinton was put in place in Arkansas where he ran a scam while governor. He was involved in the drug-trade belonging to Rome, co-working with George W. Bush and Ronald Reagan - both Jesuit-trained presidents. Then Clinton became president of the United States – under the complete and total power of the Jesuit Order as they ruled him from Georgetown University. He never resisted doing anything for the Secret Society. He was untouchable then, and even today, he can commit any crime, any act of evil, and never be prosecuted.

The Jesuit Order controls elections and can over-ride the people's votes with their power. Anyone who has said elections are *rigged*, are correct in such their presumption.

**Presidency of Bill Clinton:** January 20, 1993 – January 20, 2001. Clinton was the first president elected after the end of the Cold War, the first Baby Boomer president, and the first Democratic president since Franklin D. Roosevelt to serve two full terms. In 1992, he defeated incumbent Republican president George H. W. Bush.

The administration began with efforts by Clinton to allow gays and lesbians to serve in the military, which culminated in a compromise known as "Don't ask, don't tell", allowing them to not have to disclose their sexual orientation. The policy remained in effect until it was repealed in 2010. Clinton became the first president to appoint open gays to his Administration, issued executive orders ending the ban on security clearance for LGBT workers and banning any job discrimination based on sexual orientation in civilian public sector employment. He dramatically increased federal funding for HIV/AIDS prevention-research-treatment. However, Clinton also signed the Defense of Marriage Act (which banned the recognition of same-sex marriages); while it came to his desk with a veto-proof majority. Clinton's failure to veto DOMA was considered by many to be a blow to the LGBT rights movement.

Throughout 1998 there was a controversy over Clinton's

relationship with a young White House intern, Monica Lewinsky. Clinton initially denied the affair while testifying in the Paula Jones sexual harassment lawsuit. The opposing lawyers asked the president about it during his deposition. He stated: *"I have never had sexual relations with Monica Lewinsky. I've never had an affair with her."* Four days later he also said, *"There is not a sexual relationship, an improper sexual relationship, or any other kind of improper relationship."*

Clinton then appeared on national television on January 26 and stated: *"Listen to me, I'm going to say this again. I did not have sexual relations with that woman, Miss Lewinsky."*

However, after it was revealed that investigators had obtained a semen-stained dress as well as testimony with Lewinsky, Clinton changed tactics and admitted that an improper relationship with Lewinsky had taken place. *"Indeed I did have a relationship with Miss Lewinsky that was not appropriate. In fact, it was wrong. It constituted a critical lapse in judgment and a personal failure on my part for which I am solely and completely responsible."*

Faced with overwhelming evidence, he apologized to the nation, agreed to pay a $25,000 court fine, settled his sexual harassment lawsuit with Paula Jones for $850,000 and was temporarily disbarred, for a period of five years, from practicing law in Arkansas and before the U.S. Supreme Court. He was not tried for perjury in a court. However, he did admit to "testifying falsely" in a carefully worded statement as part of a deal to avoid indictment for perjury.

On December 19, 1998 – the lame duck session after the 1998 elections – the Republican-controlled House voted to impeach Clinton. After an impeachment trial in the Senate, the Senate voted to fully acquit Clinton in a 50-50 vote; 67 votes were required to remove Clinton from office. All

Democrats and five Republican Senators voted to fully acquit Clinton. He issued 141 pardons and 36 commutations on his last day in office on January 20. Most of the controversy surrounded Marc Rich and allegations that Hillary Clinton's brother, Hugh Rodham, accepted payments in return for influencing the president's decision-making regarding the pardons. Some of Clinton's pardons remain a point of controversy.

He left office with the highest end-of-justice approval rating for a U.S. president since World War II, but he was the first U.S. president to be impeached since Andrew Johnson (mainly as a result of the Monica Lewinsky scandal) and only the second in the U.S. history. Like Lyndon B. Johnson, however, he was acquitted by the Senate. *(Source: Wikipedia)*

**Former President Bill Clinton**

*No one can serve two masters. Either he will hate the one and love the other, or he will be devoted to the one and despise the other. You cannot serve both God and money.* **Matthew 6:24**

## *The Clinton Foundation*

The Clinton Foundation was founded in 1997 as the William J. Clinton Foundation, and called during 2013-14 the **Bill, Hillary & Chelsea Clinton Foundation** and is a non-profit corporation under section 501c (3) of the U.S. tax code. It was established by former President Bill Clinton with the stated mission to *"strengthen the capacity of people throughout the world to meet the challenges of global interdependence."* Its offices are located in New York City and Little Rock, Arkansas.

The *Clinton Global Initiative* was founded in 2005 by President Bill Clinton. Doug Band, who was a key architect of Clinton's post-presidency, was heavily involved in the formation as well. Band left his paid position at CGI in 2010 preferring to emphasize his Teneo business and family pursuits, but remains on the CGI advisory board. The overlap between CGI and Teneo, which Bill Clinton was a paid advisor with for a while, has drawn criticism at times. Teneo Holdings is a global consulting firm with deep Clinton connections. It serves as a type of private-enterprise satellite to Clinton, Inc. ***Huma Abedin***, Hillary Clinton's body-woman, was a senior advisor to Teneo at the same time she held a top position as part of Hillary's inner circle at the State Department. Co-founder and CEO is Declan Kelly who is the brains behind this operation. He served as U.S. Economic Envoy to Northern Ireland from September 2009 to May 2011.

After Hillary Clinton's appointment as Secretary of State in January 2009, she proposed hiring long-time Clinton friend and confidant, Sidney Blumenthal, as an advisor. However, Obama's chief of staff, Rahm Emanuel, blocked Blumenthal's appointment at the State Department and he was subsequently hired by the Clinton Foundation. After the 2011 uprising in Libya against Muammar Gaddafi, Blumenthal prepared from public and other sources about 25 memos which he sent as **emails to Clinton** in 2011 and 2012 with advice regarding Libyan matters.

Through 2016 the foundation had raised an estimate $2,000,000,000 from U.S. corporations, foreign governments and corporations, political donors, and various other groups and individuals. The acceptance of funds from wealthy donors has been controversial at times. The foundation "has won accolades from philanthropy experts" and has drawn bipartisan support, with members of the George W. Bush administration often participating in its programs. (The Bush and Clinton families are biologically related)

Charitable grants are not a major focus of the Clinton Foundation, which instead keeps most of its money in house and hires staff to carry out its own humanitarian programs. Because of this unusual structure for a foundation, *Charity Navigator*, a charity watchdog, has said it does not have a methodology to rate the Clinton Foundation.

In 2011, Chelsea Clinton was taking a dominant role in the foundation and had a seat on its board. To raise money for the Foundation, she gave paid speeches, such as her $65,000 address in 2014 at the University of Missouri in Kansas City for the opening of the Starr Women's Hall of Fame.

In 2013, Hillary Clinton joined the foundation following her tenure as Secretary of State. She planned to focus her work on issues regarding women and children, as well as economic development. Accordingly, at that point, it was re-named the **"Bill, Hillary & Chelsea Clinton Foundation."**

On February 18, 2015, The Washington Post reported that, *"the foundation has won accolades from philanthropy experts and has drawn bipartisan support, with members of the George W. Bush administration often participating in its programs."*

In August 2016, The Boston Globe's editorial board suggested that the Clinton Foundation cease accepting donations. The Globe's editorial board offered praise for the foundation's work but added that *"as long as either of the Clintons are in public office, or actively seeking it, they should not operate a charity, too,"* basing on the premise it represents a conflict of interest and a political distraction.

In 2016, the Reuters wire news service reported that the Clinton Foundation suspected that it had been the target of a cyber security breach, which has been described as sharing similarities with cyberattacks that targeted other institutions such as the Democratic National Committee.

### *Clinton Foundation Theory:*

- Let's begin with a separate foreign "charity". In this case, one in Canada.
- Foreign oligarchs and governments - donate to the Canadian charity. In this case, over 1000 did, contributing mega millions, probably out of the

goodness of their hearts and expected nothing in return. (Imagine Putin's comrades waking up one morning and just deciding to send untold millions to a Canadian charity).

- The Canadian charity then bundles the separate donations and makes a massive donation to the Clinton Foundation.
- The Clinton Foundation and the co-operating Canadian charity claim Canadian law prohibits the identification of individual donors.
- The Clinton Foundation then "spends" some of this money for legitimate good works programs. Unfortunately, experts believe this is on the order of 10%. Much of the balance goes to enrich the Clintons, pay salaries to untold numbers of those remaining, and fund lavish travel, etc. Again, virtually all tax-free, which means you and I are subsidizing it.
- The Clinton Foundation, with access to the world's best accountants, somehow fails to report much of this on their tax filings. They discover these "clerical errors" and begin the process of re-filing five years of tax returns after it was disclosed in *"Clinton Cash: The Untold Story of How and Why Foreign Governments and Businesses Helped Make Bill and Hillary Rich,"* by Peter Schweizer, published April 2015.
- Net result – foreign money, much of it from other countries, goes into the Clintons' pockets tax free and untraceable back to the original donor, which is best known as ***money laundering.***
- The Canadian "charity" includes as a principal one Frank Giustra – the one who was central to the information of Uranium One, the Canadian

company that somehow acquired massive U.S. uranium interests and then sold them to an organization controlled by Russia. This transaction required U.S. State Department approval, and Secretary of State Clinton granted the request.

- This is massive in comparison to Virginia Governor Bob McDonnell and his wife who took $165,000 in gifts and loans for doing minor favors for a man who was promoting a vitamin company. Of course, that was not legal, but not exactly putting U.S. security at risk.

The Clinton Foundation is currently under investigation stemming from rumors of the conflict of interest of the State Department and the Clinton funding.

*For the love of money is a root of all kinds of evil. Some people, eager for money, have wandered from the faith and pierced themselves with many griefs.*
**1 Timothy 6:10**

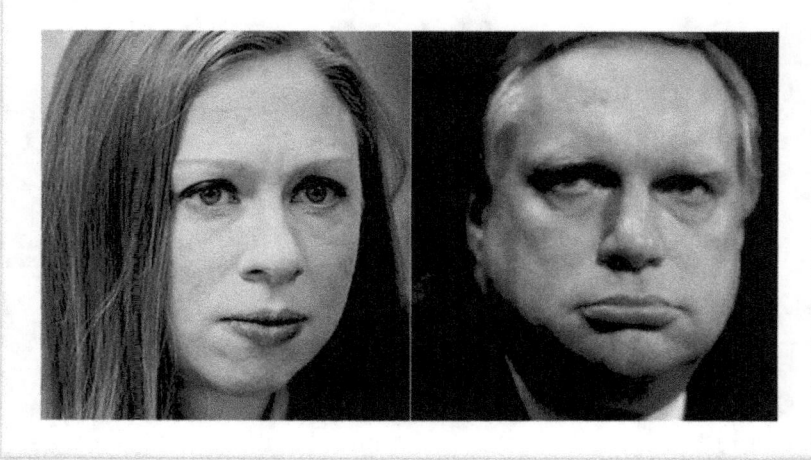

**Chelsea Clinton Mezvinsky has a striking resemblance to Webster Hubbell who was once her mother's law partner at the Rose Law Firm in Arkansas.**

## *Barack Hussein Obama II*

Barack Hussein Obama, II was born August 4, 1961 in Honolulu, Hawaii. People who express doubts about Obama's birthplace are often informally called "birthers", a term that parallels the nickname "truthers". Wikipedia states that Obama was born at the Medical Center for Women and Children in Honolulu, Hawaii to Ann Dunham from Wichita, Kansas, and Barack Obama, Sr., a Luo from Nyang'oma Kogelo, Nyanza Province (in what was then the Colony and Protectorate of Kenya), who was attending the University of Hawaii. Obama's parents were divorced in 1964. He attended kindergarten in 1966-1967 at Noelene Elementary School in Honolulu. In 1967, his mother married Indonesian student Lolo Soetoro, who was also attending the University of Hawaii, and the family moved to Jakarta, Indonesia where Obama attended the Catholic St. Francis of Assisi School before transferring to State Elementary School Menteng, an elite Indonesian public school in Menteng. As a child in Indonesia, Obama was called "Barry", sometimes Barry Soetoro, reflecting his step-father's surname, and sometimes Barry Obama, using his father's surname.

For about two years starting in 1969, Obama's mother had employed a "Waria" or transgender woman named Turdi (later changed to Evie). Turdi was originally hired as a cook after having met him at a cocktail party, but it didn't take long before he was also eight-year old Barry's caretaker, playing with him and bringing him to and from school. Turdi had always seen himself as a woman trapped inside his male body. As Evie, he would dress as a drag queen and tried to not do so in front of the young boy. However, he would make Barry laugh when he put on his mother's lipstick. After he put the boy to bed, he would dress in his female attire, apply makeup, and leave the house to socialize with other drag queens, transvestites, prostitutes, and transgenders who were called Fantastic Dolls.

In keeping with Indonesia's relaxed attitudes toward homosexuality, "Evie" carried on an affair with a local butcher, as told by his longtime residents in an article by the Associated Press and New York Times. As fixtures of Jakarta's streetscape, they would entertain people by dancing and playing volleyball.

According to Wikipedia, LGBT people in Jakarta are legally labeled as "CACAT", which means 'mentally handicapped and therefore not protected under the law'. The Islamic Indonesian Ulema Council ruled that transgender people must not seek gender reassignment surgery. A Muslim clinic from the Council said, "If they are not willing to cure themselves medically and religiously," they must be willing to "accept their fate to be ridiculed and harassed." The Council believe their obligation to society is reproduction.

In the summer of 1970, Obama returned to Hawaii for an

extended visit with his maternal grandparents, Stanley and Madelyn Dunham (relatives of the George Bush families). On August 15, 1970, Dunham and Soetoro celebrated the birth of their daughter, Maya Kassandra Soetoro. In mid-1971, Obama moved back to Hawaii to live with his grandparents and attend Punahou School starting in 5th grade. In December 1971, the boy was visited for a month by his father, Barack Obama, Sr. from Kenya. It was the last time Obama would see his father. This was followed by his mother visiting her son and parents in Honolulu from late 1971 to January 1972. From 6th grade through 8th grade at Punahou, Obama lived with his mother and half-sister, Maya.

He moved to California in 1979 at age 18 to attend Occidental College for two years after graduation from high school in Hawaii. He then transferred to Columbia University in New York from 1981-1983 graduating with a BA in Political Science. His transcripts have not been made publicly available. Obama entered Harvard Law School at age 27 and attended from 1988-1991. He graduated with a JD degree in 1991. While at Harvard, he served on the board of the Black Law Students Association, and was elected President of the Harvard Law Review in spring 1990. His transcripts have not been made publicly available.

Passages taken from Obama's 1995 memoir, *"Dreams from My Father: A Story of Race and Inheritance,"* reveal his use of drugs while in college. "Pot had helped, and booze; maybe a little blow when you could afford it," wrote Obama.

Others have reported that Obama had used a lot of cocaine and often frequented the gay community – even while serving in the Illinois State Senate 1996-2004.

There was the reported incidence when Lawrence "Larry" Wayne Sinclair flew to Chicago on November 3,

1999 to attend the graduation of his best friend's son from basic training at the Great Lakes Navy Training Center. On November 6, Sinclair, a homosexual, asked the driver of Five Star Limo if he knew anyone who wanted to 'socialize' and show him around Chicago. The driver knew what he meant and made a call to his friend, Barack Obama, the Illinois state senator, and arranged a meeting.

They met at an upscale Chicago area bar in Gurnee, Illinois. Sinclair remembered the bar as "Alibis". He asked if Obama could obtain cocaine and the state senator allegedly made a call from his cell phone to make the purchase. They left the bar and drove to an unknown location where Obama allegedly purchased cocaine for $250 paid by Larry Sinclair who also claims Obama purchased crack cocaine for himself. Then they engaged in consensual sex and used cocaine while in the rented limo.

Barack Obama had his name on two bills of record but was absent from the Illinois Senate opening session on November 4, 1999. When questioned by Tim Russert of the *Chicago Tribune* reference releasing his records for that date, and his reason for missing the session, he skirted the issue offering his defense in this manner: "The problem is whatever remaining documents I have are inevitably incomplete... I don't want to mislead people. I don't know the extent of the records that I have as a state senator."

Sinclair later filed a lawsuit in Minnesota District Court, claiming the Obama staff made threats and attempts of intimidation against him. He published his book, *"**Barrack Obama and Larry Sinclair: Cocaine, Sex, Lies & Murder?**"* which still remains on Amazon.com.

Drew Harwell, journalist for Independent Florida Alligator, wrote: "Obama's confessions are a far cry from those of the White House's last Democrat, former President Bill Clinton, whose testimony that he 'experimented with marijuana a time or two' but didn't inhale and never tried the drug again became a national punch line.

Obama has even gotten in on the joke himself. In a 2006 speech to the American Society of Magazine Editors, the candidate said, 'Look, you know, when I was a kid, I inhaled. Frequently. That was the point!'

President George W. Bush has dealt with drug issues as well. In addition to his open admission of alcohol abuse during his college years and a drunken driving arrest at the age of 30, Bush has also faced allegations of cocaine use.

But unlike Obama, Bush has sidestepped the charges and remains obtuse on his history, calling his youth 'irresponsible' and insisting he's made mistakes but offering no further details."

Barack Hussein Obama (2008-2016) was the first multi-racial and alleged *gay* man to be elected as President of the United States in 2008 after having defeated the former first lady, Hillary, wife of former President Bill Clinton. He served 1993-2001. Both presidents served two terms in the White House. President George W. Bush served from 2000-2008)

President Barack Hussein Obama once quoted, "Whatever we were, we are no longer a Christian nation," and he has mocked our Holy Bible saying, "The Sermon on the Mount is a passage that is so radical that our defense department would not survive its application."

President Obama is thought by many to have been hand-picked by the **Illuminati** to either bring down the United States or to usher in a fascist police state through socialist laws and staged conflicts. Virtually every action he has taken has been analyzed for **Illuminati** influence, with others believing he is either an agent of Satan or an antichrist.

*Dear children, do not let anyone lead you astray. He who does what is right is righteous, just as he is righteous. He who does what is sinful is of the devil, because the devil has been sinning from the beginning. The reason the Son of God appeared was to destroy the devil's work.*
**1 John 3:7-8**

**President Barack Obama and The Pope**

## *"Rules for Radicals"*
Dedicated to Lucifer by Saul Alinsky (1909-1972)

Reference Hillary Clinton, Dr. Ben Carson on the night of the Republican National Convention, was quoted as saying: "Let me tell you something about Saul Alinsky. He wrote a book called *'Rules for Radicals'*. On the dedication page, it acknowledges Lucifer, the original radical who gained his own kingdom. Now, think about that. This is a nation where our founding document, the Declaration of Independence, talks about certain inalienable rights that come from our Creator. This is a nation where every coin in our pocket and every bill in our wallet says, 'In God we Trust'. So are we willing to elect someone as president who has as their role model somebody who acknowledges Lucifer?"

Therefore, let us take a look at the dedication Saul Alinsky put in his handbook: "Lest we forget at least an over-the-shoulder acknowledgment to the very first radical: from all our legends, mythology, and history...the first radical known to man who rebelled against the establishment and did it so effectively that he at least won his own kingdom ~ Lucifer."

The American Left is trying to destroy our nation in hopes of building a new one by undermining its core values. It was Alinsky who wrote, "Do one of three things. One, go find a wailing wall and feel sorry for yourselves. Two, go psycho and start bombing – but this will only swing people to the right. Three, learn a lesson. Go home, organize, build power and at the next convention, you be the delegates."

The strategy of working within the system until you can accumulate enough power to destroy it was what radicals in the 60's called "boring from within"...like termites, they set about to eat away at the foundations of the building in expectation that one day they could cause it to collapse.

Hillary Clinton and Barack Obama are students of Alinsky's methods. Hillary had met Alinsky at a Methodist church outing when she was a teenager. They were impressed with one another. In late 1968, Alinsky offered Hillary Rodham a job working for him. She had aspirations and wrote her senior thesis on Alinsky in 1969, "There is Only the Fight...": An Analysis of the Alinsky Model. While he believed the system could only be changed from the outside, she believed it could be changed from the inside. She, along with others, took Alinsky's "radical" methods and made them mainstream.

Seventeen years later, in 1985, another young honor student was offered a job as an organizer in Chicago. By then, Alinsky had died, but a group of his disciples hired **Barack Obama**, a 23-year old Columbia University graduate, to organize black residents on the South Side, while learning and applying Alinsky's philosophy of street-value democracy. The recruiter called the $13,000-a-year job *very romantic* – until you do it.

(Article contributed by Gary DeMar, an American writer, lecturer and former president of an American Christian nonprofit organization. He earned his Ph.D. in Christian Intellectual History from Whitefield Theological Seminary in 2007).

**Note:** Barack Obama's paternal grandfather, born 1922, married his third wife, Sarah Onyango Hussein Obama. Although not blood-related, Barack Obama called her "Granny Sarah". A strong believer of the Islamic faith, she reminded everyone that Obama's grandfather had been a Muslim.

**Note:** Malik Obama, the older half-brother of Senator Barack Obama, Illinois, gave a brief interview to Israeli Army Radio. He was quoted as saying: "My brother will be a good president for the Jews. If elected, he will be a good president for the Jewish people, despite his Muslim background."

Barack Obama is truly **not** the President of the United States. He is **not** a powerful person at all. Rather, he is a front man for more powerful entities that hide in the shadows. The real power in the world is not the United States, or even China. As previously mentioned, the **Roman Catholic Church (Vatican)** is the single most powerful "evil force" in the world as God will allow it to be through His divine authority.

*Then Jesus came to them and said, "All authority in heaven and on Earth has been given to me."*
**Matthew 28:18**

**President Barack Obama**

**The man who will do anything possible to have a THIRD TERM as President in the White House.**

## *Michelle LaVaughn Robinson Obama*

As unbelievable as any conspiracy rumors can be, when placed alongside all the other unbelievable wicked and supernatural things happening to this nation, one can be brought to expect more of such implausible madness when hearing the First Lady could possibly be a **"man"**.

In a speech on September 30, 2011 (you can research online), at the transition or change-of-office ceremony of the Chairman of the Joint Chiefs of Staff at Fort Myer, Virginia, Obama referred to his wife not as Michelle, but as *Michael.* In playing this video over and over, I am certain this is not a voice-over.

Obama clearly said: "Distinguished guests, men and women of the finest military in the world, most of all, Admiral Mullen, Deborah, *Michael and I* also want to acknowledge your son, Jack who was deployed today, all of you have performed extraordinary service to our country..."

Michelle Obama, First Lady of the U.S., was allegedly born *Michael LaVaughn Robinson* in Chicago, Illinois on January 17, 1964. The second child was allegedly born to

Fraser Robinson III, a well-known cocaine dealer and union thug for Crime Lord/Major Richard J. Daley, and Marian Shields Robinson, a transient street prostitute who was diagnosed with the HIV virus in 1998. He (Michael) was a popular high school athlete and in 1982 accepted a scholarship to play middle linebacker for the Oregon State Beavers.

After finishing a respectable rookie season with 88 tackles and 7.5 sacks, he suddenly dropped out of the school. Fellow teammates observed that Robinson could regularly be heard lamenting over how he is a "woman trapped inside a man's body", and on January 13, 1983, he underwent sex reassignment surgery at Johns Hopkins University School of Medicine. To hide the shame of his new identity, Michael left Oregon State to attend Princeton University under his new legal name, **"Michelle Robinson"**. Years later, he met Barry Obama, Jr., a Kenyan immigrant who later became aware of "Michelle's" true identity. They subsequently married and ***adopted two children.*** *(Source: An anonymous former White House staff member of the Obama administration and former member of the First Lady's personal staff).*

A video online systematically argues that physical traits, including Michelle's fingers, shoulders, neck muscles, head-to-body ratio and trace of an Adam's apple, all point to her being a biological male. There are no pictures of a pregnant Michelle, nor has anyone found birth records of "her" two daughters.

On July 3, 2014, after officiating at a wedding of two homosexuals in New York, comedienne Joan Rivers was asked by an off-camera reporter: "Do you think the country...United States will see the first gay president or first woman president?

Joan Rivers answered, sounding wary and definitely not

in a joking mood: "We already have the first gay president with Obama, so let's just calm down. You know Michelle is a tranny...a transgender. We all know."

Two months almost to the day of Joan Rivers' allegations of the Obamas on September 4, she was declared dead after she had stopped breathing during a routine endoscopy in a clinic.

Her daughter, Melissa Rivers, later appeared on a special television episode and shared a personal handwritten note she had received from President Barack Obama, which read in part: *"...not only did she make us laugh, she made us think."*

The Sidney Morning Herald reported that just weeks before her passing, Ms. Rivers told the Sunday Times Magazine in an interview that Mrs. Obama was not allowed to attend her funeral because she was a "tranny." Other banned celebrities included late-night host Chelsea Handler and singer Adele for different reasons.

This is all a "conspiracy theory" and other than viewing the physical characteristics of the First Lady of the White House, there is no substantial evidence to support this alleged theory.

**Barry Obama and Michelle aka "Michael"**

*For certain men whose condemnation was written about long ago have secretly slipped in among you. They are godless men, who change the grace of our God into a license for immorality and deny Jesus Christ our only Sovereign and Lord.* **Jude 1:4**

## *Who is Julian Assange and what part does he play in this 2016 political conspiracy?*

Julian Paul Assange was born July 3, 1971 and is an Australian computer programmer, publisher and journalist. He is editor-in-chief of the organization **WikiLeaks**, which he founded in 2006. His mother was a visual artist and his father an anti-war activist and builder. His un-married parents had separated before he was born. When he was a year old, his mother married Richard Brett Assange, an actor, with whom she ran a small theatre company. They divorced around 1979.

In 1987 Assange began hacking under the name Mendax. He and two others - known as "Trax" and "Prime Suspect" – formed a hacking group they called the *International Subversives.* During this time he hacked into the Pentagon and other US Department of Defense facilities, MILNET, the US Navy, NASA, and Australia's Overseas Telecommunications Commission; Citibank, Lockheed Martin, Motorola, Panasonic, and Xerox, and the Australian

National University, La Trobe University, and Stanford University's SRI International. He is thought to have been involved in the WANK hack at NASA in 1989, but he does not acknowledge this.

In 1994, he was charged with 31 counts of hacking and related crimes. In December 1996, he pled guilty to 25 charges (the other six were dropped), was ordered to pay a restitution and released on a good behavior bond, avoiding a heavier penalty due to the perceived absence of malicious or mercenary intent and his disrupted childhood. After the trial, Assange lived in Melbourne where he survived on single-parent income support.

Since November 2010, Assange has been subject to extradition to Sweden where he is wanted for questioning over two counts of sexual molestation - one count of unlawful coercion and one count of "lesser-degree rape", after having met two different women while on his visit to Sweden. He continues to deny the allegations. The year 2010 culminated with the Sam Adams Award, which Assange accepted in October, and a string of distinctions in December.

After exhausting his legal options in the United Kingdom of Great Britain and Northern Ireland, Assange failed to surrender for extradition. Instead, he sought and was granted asylum by the Republic of Ecuador in August 2012. He has since remained in the Embassy of Ecuador in London, and is unable to leave without being arrested for breaching his bail conditions. UK Foreign Secretary Philip Hammond said the claim was "ridiculous" and that the group was "made up of lay people", and called Assange a *fugitive from justice.*

WikiLeaks has published secret information, news leaks, and classified media from anonymous sources. By 2015 WikiLeaks had published more than 10 million documents and associated analyses, and was described by Assange himself as "a giant library of the world's most persecuted documents".

U.S. Vice-President Joe Biden called Julian Assange a "terrorist". Some called for his assassination or execution. However, he has received support from high officials and dignitaries who have come to his defense throughout various countries  - Brazil, Ecuador, Russia, Britain, Spain, and Argentina.

Assange wrote on WikiLeaks in February 2016: *"I have had years of experience dealing with Hillary Clinton and have read thousands of her cables. Hillary lacks judgment and will push the U.S. into endless, stupid wars which spread terrorism...she certainly should not become president of the United States."*

On July 22, 2016, WikiLeaks released emails and files sent from or received by the Democratic National Committee (DNC). The New York Times reported that *"Assange accused Mrs. Clinton of having been among those pushing to indict him..."* and that he had timed the release to coincide with the 2016 Democratic National Convention. In an interview with Robert Preston of *ITV New*, Assange suggested that he saw Hillary Clinton as a personal foe. He said in an interview with "Democracy Now!" that choosing between Donald Trump and Hillary Clinton is like choosing between cholera or gonorrhea. "Personally, I would prefer neither."

***Why I Created WikiLeaks' Searchable Database of 30,000 Emails from Clinton's Private Server... (Source: Democracy Now online interview by Juan Gonzalez with Julian Assange – July 25, 2016)***

***Juan Gonzalez:*** "Julian, I want to mention something

else. In March, you launched a searchable archive for over 30,000 emails and email attachments sent to and from Hillary Clinton's private email server while she was secretary of state. The 50,547 pages of documents span the time from June 2010 to August 2014; 7,500 of the documents were sent by Hillary Clinton herself. The emails were made available in the form of thousands of PDF's by the U.S. Department as the result of a Freedom of Information Act request. Why did you do this and what's the importance, from your perspective, of being able to create a searchable base?"

***Julian Assange:*** "Well, WikiLeaks has become the rebel library of Alexandria. It is the single most significant collection of information that doesn't exist elsewhere, in a searchable, accessible, citable form, about how modern institutions actually behave. And it's gone on to set people free from prison, where documents have been used in their court cases; hold the CIA accountable for renditions programs; feed into election cycles, which have resulted in the termination of, in some case – or contributed to the termination of governments, in some cases, taken the heads of intelligence agencies, ministers of defense of what our civilization is. We can't possibly hope to reform that which we do not understand.

So, those Hillary Clinton emails, they connect together with the cables that we have published of Hillary Clinton, creating a rich picture of how Hillary Clinton performs in office, but, more broadly, how the U.S. Department of State operates. So, for example, the disastrous, absolutely disastrous intervention in Libya, the destruction of the Gaddafi government, which led to the occupation of ISIS of large segments of that country, weapons flows going over to Syria, being pushed by Hillary Clinton, into Jihadists within Syria, including ISIS, that's there in those emails.

There's more than 1,700 emails in Hillary Clinton's collection, that we have released, just about Libya alone."

*He changes times and seasons; He sets up kings and deposes them. He gives wisdom to the wise and knowledge to the discerning.* **Daniel 2:21**

**Julian Paul Assange - WikiLeaks**

*You intended to harm me, but God intended it for good to accomplish what is now being done, the saving of many lives.* **Genesis 50:20**

Since I entered politics, I have chiefly had men's views confided to me privately. Some of the biggest men in the United States, in the Field of commerce and manufacture, are afraid of something. They know that there is a power somewhere - so organized, so subtle, so watchful, so interlocked, so complete, so pervasive - that they better not speak above their breath when they speak in condemnation of it.

(Woodrow Wilson)

izquotes.com

## *President Woodrow Wilson*

## *Timeline:*

**1964** – Hillary worked on the presidential campaign of Republican candidate Barry Goldwater and proudly announced, "I'm a Goldwater girl!"

**1968** – Hillary switched to the Democratic Party and campaigned for Eugene McCarthy.

**1970** – Hillary worked as a summer intern for civil rights lawyer Marian Wright Edelman.

**1973-1974** – Hillary worked as an attorney for the Children's Defense Fund.

**January, 1974** – Hillary began working for John Doar, the special counsel to the House Judiciary Committee who was in charge of the inquiry into the possible impeachment of President Richard Nixon.

**August, 1974** – Hillary moved to Arkansas to teach at the University of Arkansas School of Law.

**1974-1977** – Hillary was Director of Legal Aid Clinic at the University of Arkansas School of Law.

**October 11, 1975** - While working as a faculty member at the Law School of the University of Arkansas, Hillary married Bill Clinton. He was also working as a faculty member at the same university.

**1974-1977 and 1979-1980** – Hillary was Assistant Professor of Law at the University of Arkansas School of Law.

**1976** - After law school, Bill was elected Attorney General of Arkansas.

**1977** – Suzanne Coleman had Bill Clinton as her law professor and reportedly had an affair with him. She died from suicide - gunshot wound to back of head.

**1976-1992** – Hillary was an attorney at Rose Law Firm, Little Rock, Arkansas. Her fellow attorneys, Webster Hubbell and Vince Foster, both helped her to become the first female partner in their firm in 1979.

**1978** – President Jimmy Carter appointed Hillary Clinton to the board of directors of the Legal Services Corp., an organization that provided federal funds to legal-aid bureaus throughout the U. S.

**1978** – Bill Clinton was elected governor of Arkansas. At 32, he was the youngest governor in the country at that time. Hillary Clinton continued to work at Rose Law Firm, making her the First Lady of Arkansas to continue working while her husband was governor.

**1979-1981** - Bill served as governor of Arkansas and again from 1983 to 1993. He was known for being a "New Democrat" while governor. During his time as governor, Clinton changed the state's school system.

**1979** – Governor Bill Clinton appointed Hillary chairperson of the Rural Health Advisory Committee, whose members would deal with the issue of providing health care in isolated areas.

**1979** – The Whitewater Development Corporation was formed by the Clintons, along with James and Susan McDougal, which developed into a scandal during Bill's term as governor.

**1980** – Governor Bill Clinton lost the 1980 gubernatorial election. He returned to office in 1982 and was re-elected in 1984, 1986, and 1990.

**1983** – Governor Bill Clinton appointed his wife to head the Arkansas Education Standards Committee.

**1988 and 1991** – Hillary Clinton was named one of the 100 most influential U.S. lawyers by the National Law Journal. When Clinton was governor of Arkansas, he let the CIA and the Contras (Barry Seal, drug dealer and pilot) bring cocaine into the U.S. through the airport in Mena, Arkansas, with President Bush's knowledge and approval. The evidence for this statement is mostly testimony from anonymous sources. This was through the longtime relationship between the Clintons and the Bushes.

The plane's pilots involved in the Iran-Contra scandal kept journals, which were later turned over by one of the wives. The written reports revealed exactly what was going on at that time in Arkansas. Governor Bill Clinton also allowed Tyson Chicken to command the state of Arkansas and federal mandates for pollution prevention, and therefore pollute the Arkansas waters. This speaks volumes about the double-talking, lying sociopaths who are praised for being such great politicians.

**1988** – Barry Seal, drug dealer in Mena, Arkansas, was shot three times with a machine gun – when in Louisiana.

**1988** – Kevin Ives and Don Henry were two boys slain and found on train tracks after coming up on a cocaine exchange, known as the "train track murders". The following seven were also murdered because of their connection:

**July, 1988** – Keith Coney's motorcycle hit the back of a truck.

**November, 1988** – Keith McMaskle was stabbed 113 times.

**April 1989** – Jeff Rhodes was shot, mutilated, and

discovered in a trash dump.

**July 1989** – Gregory Collins was killed by gunshots.

**July 1989** – Richard Winters was killed as suspect in a robbery set-up.

**1989** – James Milan was found with his head decapitated. Officials tried to say his dog stole his head and ate it.

**June, 1990** – Jordan Kettleson was shot to death while sitting in his truck.

**August 10, 1991** – Danny Casolaro slit his wrists in a hotel in West Virginia.

**1992** – Bill Clinton was elected president.

**July 30, 1992** – C. Victor Raiser, former National Finance Co-Chairman of Clinton for President, and also Montgomery Raiser (his son), both died in a private plane crash in Alaska on a fishing trip. Mr. Raiser was considered to be a major player on the Clinton team.

**September 24, 1992** – Paul Tully, DNC Political Director, was found dead in a Little Rock, Arkansas hotel room. He was a key member of the damage control squad and came up with some of the Clinton strategies.

**December 7, 1992** – Paula Grober, Clinton's interpreter for the deaf, traveled with Clinton from 1978 until 1992, when she was killed later in a one-car accident with no witnesses.

**January 1993** – The president named Hillary Clinton to lead the Task Force on National Health Care Reform.

**February 23, 1993** - Jarrett Robertson, Col. William Densberger, Col. Robert Kelly, and Spec. Gary Rhodes all died when their Army UH-60 Blackhawk helicopter crashed on landing in Wiesbaden, Germany. A jury later found that the helicopter "entered into an uncontrollable right turn caused by a design defect!"

**February 28, 1993** – Steve Willis, Robert Williams, Todd McKeehan, and Conway LeBleu were Alcohol, Tobacco and Firearms agents killed during the Waco confrontation.

**May 19, 1993** – John (James) Wilson, former Washington, D.C. council member, had ties to Whitewater. He died in a suicide hanging.

**May 19, 1993** – Sgt. Brian Haney, Sgt. Timothy Sabel, Maj. William Barkley, and Capt. Scott Reynolds died in a helicopter crash. They were members of Marine Helicopter Squadron One, the unit responsible for transporting the President. They died when the Blackhawk helicopter they had taken out for a maintenance-evaluation flight crashed.

**June 22, 1993** – Paul Wilcher, an attorney investigating corruption, federal elections, drug and gun smuggling through Mena, the Waco incident, and had just delivered a lengthy report to Janet Reno, was discovered dead on the toilet in Washington, D.C. According to the Washington Times, Wilcher was investigating the theory of an 'October Surprise' conspiracy during the 1980 federal election campaign. He had been interviewing an inmate who claimed to have piloted George Bush to Paris so he could secretly seek to delay the release of 52 American hostages in Iran.

This would have been a key political advantage for Clinton, just a year into his first term, to bump off someone who was supposedly about to dig up some major dirt on the opposition party. However, the Clintons and the Bushes were close friends, and as mentioned before, cousins.

**July 7, 1993** – Vince Foster, Clinton White House Council, was found dead in Ft. Marcy Park in Washington, D.C. He supposedly killed himself with a shotgun, and was found a few days later with a suitcase that contained a shredded suicide note. Foster knew the Clintons from his time at Rose Law Firm in Arkansas, and had intimate details of the Clintons' financial situation. Apparently, he made a phone call to Hillary Clinton just hours before his death. The person who found him never saw a gun.

**August 15, 1993** – Jon Parnell Walker, Resolution Trust Corp. investigator mysteriously fell from an apartment balcony at the Lincoln Towers in Arlington, Virginia.

**September 10, 1993** - Dr. Stanley Heard, the Clinton family chiropractor, died in a plane crash. His personal small plane developed problems so he rented another resulting in fire breaking out in flight, and he crashed. Also with him was Steve Dickson, his personal attorney.

**John Hillier**, video journalist and investigator, who helped to produce the documentaries "Circle of Power" and "The Clinton Chronicles" mysteriously died in a dentist's chair for no apparent reason.

**September 26, 1993** – Luther "Jerry" Parks, a former security team member for Governor Clinton, had compiled an extensive file on Clinton's activities. His family had reported he was being followed and his home was broken into just before being gunned down as he left a Mexican restaurant at the edge of Little Rock. His murder remains unsolved.

**September 28, 1993** – Hillary Clinton testified before the House Ways and Means Committee in support of President Clinton's health care package. The health care reform bill was later defeated by Congress.

**November 29, 1993** – Ed Willey, a former state senator, lawyer, and then a Clinton fund raiser was said to have committed suicide by the use of a shotgun to the head while in the woods in Virginia. He had served as a volunteer in the White House Social Office.

**1993** – James Bunch, in Arkansas, had possession of a "little black book" and committed suicide by the use of a shotgun. At the same time he was killing himself, his wife was allegedly being groped by Bill Clinton. She said she had gone to the Chief Executive looking for a job to help her family of a financial crisis and found herself fending off his advances.

Clinton admitted to the meeting but denied her version of what took place. Kathleen Willey testified in Paula Jones' sexual harassment suit against Clinton.

**March 1, 1994** – Hershel Friday, a Clinton fund-raiser, died in a mysterious plane crash.

**March 3, 1994** – Dr. Donald Rogers, dentist, was killed in a plane crash on his way to an interview with reporter Ambrose Evans-Pritchard to reveal information about Clinton.

Johnny Lawhorn, Jr. found a check to Bill Clinton in trunk of his car left at his mechanic shop. Later, he died when his car hit a utility pole.

**May 11, 1994** – Kathy Ferguson, former wife of Arkansas State Trooper Danny Ferguson, the co-defendant with Bill Clinton in the Paula Jones lawsuit was found dead at the home of her boyfriend, Bill Shelton. She died from a gunshot wound to the head. They discovered her packed suitcases at the door.

**June 11, 1994** – Bill Shelton, Arkansas State Trooper (Kathy Ferguson's boyfriend), died from suicide – gunshot wound.

**June 23, 1994** – Stanley Huggins, a lawyer investigating Madison Guaranty was said to have died from a suicide but examiner said he had pneumonia.

**July 8, 1994** – Gandy Baugh, attorney for Dan Lasater in a financial misconduct case, supposedly jumped out the window of a tall building to commit suicide.

**October 23, 1994** – Florence Martin of Mabelle, Texas and an accountant for the CIA, had information on the Barry Seal case. She died from three gunshot wounds to the head.

**April 3, 1996** – Ron Brown died in plane crash but autopsy showed round bullet hole in top of skull. Charles Meissner, Assistant Secretary of Commerce, died also, along with John Huang who had been given a special security clearance by Meissner.

**November 29, 1996** – Barbara Wise worked with Ron Bean. She was found locked in her office inside a closet bruised and half nude – dead!

**1996** – Bill Clinton defeated Bob Dole in the 1996 election. President Clinton was sued by Paula Jones for sexual harassment, but the lawsuit was officially dismissed after Jones failed to prove damages. This made Clinton the first sitting U.S. president to be sued.

**July 6, 1997** – Mary Mahoney, former White House intern, was gunned down in a coffee shop. Nothing was taken. It was suspected that she was to testify about sexual harassment in the White House.

**March 8, 1998** – James McDougal, a key witness for Whitewater prosecutors when the investigation centered on an Arkansas land deal in which the president and McDougal were involved, had a pre-existing heart condition and died of a heart attack while in solitary confinement at the Federal Medical Center prison in Fort Worth.

**December 1998** – President Clinton was accused of wrongdoing by the U.S. House of Representatives during the Monica Lewinsky scandal.

**February 6, 2000** – Hillary Clinton announced her candidacy for the U.S. Senate.

**2000** – Charles Ruff was one of Clinton's attorneys during the impeachment trial and was known to have inside information on the White House e-mail scandal as well. Original reports were that he died in an accident in his home although no details were given. Then the report changed to claim that he was found in his bedroom unconscious, and declared dead on arrival at the hospital. The authorities will provide no details other than the usual assurance there was no foul play involved.

**May 16, 2000** – Hillary Clinton accepted the nomination of the New York State Democratic Party for the U.S. Senate.

**September 20, 2000** – Independent counsel Robert Ray announced that the evidence found in the Whitewater case was insufficient to prove that the Clintons knowingly participated in any criminal conduct.

**November 7, 2000** – Hillary Clinton was elected to the U.S. Senate with 56% of the vote.

**February 13, 2001** – Hillary Clinton made her first address on the floor of the Senate.

**June 9, 2003** – Hillary Clinton released her memoir, "Living History". The book sold over 200,000 copies on its first day of release.

**November 7, 2006** – Hillary Clinton was re-elected for a second term.

**January 20, 2007** – Hillary Clinton announced she was creating an exploratory committee for the 2008 presidential race.

**January 8, 2008** – Hillary Clinton won the New Hampshire Democratic primary with 39% of the vote.

**June 7, 2008** – Hillary Clinton suspended her presidential campaign and endorsed Barack Obama.

**August 27, 2008** – Hillary Clinton was formally nominated as a candidate for president at the Democratic National Convention in Denver, Colorado. She received 341 votes before interrupting the roll call to ask that Obama be nominated by acclamation.

**January 21, 2009** – Hillary Clinton was confirmed as Secretary of State.

**June 2009** – Hillary Clinton fell in the basement of the State Department as she was walking to her car and broke her arm, which required surgery.

**October 15, 2012** – During an interview with CNN, Hillary Clinton took responsibility for the attack on the U.S. consulate in Benghazi, Libya. She claimed as head of the State Department the security of more than 60,000 people in 275 posts as her responsibility.

**December 15, 2012** – Hillary Clinton sustained a concussion after becoming dehydrated and fainting.

**December 30, 2012** – Hillary Clinton was hospitalized after doctors discovered a blood clot during a follow-up exam related to the concussion. Doctors announced on December 31st that the clot was located in-between Clinton's brain and skull, but they were confident she would make a full recovery.

**January 2, 2013** – Hillary Clinton was released from the hospital.

**January 23, 2013** – Secretary Clinton testified for more than five hours before the House Foreign Affairs Committee and the Senate Foreign Relations Committee.

**February 1, 2013** – Hillary Clinton resigned as Secretary of State.

**March 18, 2013** – Hillary Clinton announced that she supported marriage rights for same-sex couples. In the 2008 presidential primaries she supported civil unions and partner benefits but not same-sex marriage.

**November 20, 2013** – Bill Clinton was awarded the Presidential Medal of Freedom, the highest civilian honor of the U.S., by President Barack Obama.

**March 2, 2015** – The New York Times reported that Hillary Clinton exclusively used a personal e-mail account during her time as Secretary of State. The account, fed through its own server, raised security and preservation concerns. The House committee investigating the attack on the U.S. consulate in Libya discovered the personal account when the Department of State, through Hillary Clinton, provided those e-mails to the committee.

**March 10, 2015** – During a press conference, Hillary Clinton said she used a private domain for her official work during her time at the State Department out of "convenience," but admitted in retrospect "it would have been better" to use multiple e-mails.

**April 12, 2015** – Hillary Clinton officially announced a second bid for the White House. The initial word came in an e-mail to supporters from John Podesta, a longtime Clinton ally, then a video launched on YouTube and a newly minted Facebook page. Shortly after declaring her candidacy for president, she resigned from the Bill, Hillary, and Chelsea Clinton Foundation's board of directors, according to foundation officials.

**June 13, 2015** – Walter Scheib was hired by the Clinton White House as a Chef and continued to serve the Bush Administration. He was reported missing during a hike, and his body was found almost two miles away at the bottom of a river. No cause of death has been made.

**August 11, 2015** – Hillary Clinton's spokesman announced that she would turn over her private e-mail server and a flash drive to Justice Department officials, as an ongoing probe into the handling of classified information continued. Inspector General Charles McCullough, III, notified Congress that two of Clinton's e-mails contained top secret materials.

**October 22, 2015** – Hillary Clinton testified for 11 hours before the congressional panel investigating the attacks on a U.S. mission in Benghazi, Libya that led to the deaths of four Americans.

**May 25, 2016** – A State Department Inspector General report stated that former Secretary of State Hillary Clinton failed to follow the rules or inform key department staff regarding her use of a private e-mail server, according to a copy of the report obtained by CNN.

**June 6, 2016** – According to CNN's delegate and super delegate count, Hillary R. Clinton had clinched the Democratic presidential nomination and would become the first woman in the history of the U.S. to lead the presidential ticket of a major political party.

**June 22, 2016** – John Ashe, a U.N. official, met his death while exercising in a gym. No one was said to have been witness to the barbell falling on his throat and crushing his larynx. It was "reported" he suffered a heart attack pending an autopsy by the Westchester medical examiner. Ashe was scheduled to testify (along with Ng Lap Seng, Chinese businessman and co-defendant) for having received more than $1 billion in donations during his term as president of the U.N. Seng had also found ways to illegally funnel money to Democrats during President Bill Clinton's term in office. A source told The Political Insider if Ashe had lived, prosecutors would have linked him to the Clinton bagman Ng lap Seng. It would have been embarrassing for them, so his death was conveniently timed.

**July 8, 2016** – Seth Conrad Rich was murdered in Washington, D.C.

**July 26, 2016** – Hillary Clinton officially became the Democratic Party nominee for President.

**July 28, 2016** – Hillary Clinton accepted the Democratic Party's nomination for President during the Democratic National Convention on Thursday, July 28, 2016.

**August 1, 2016** – Victor Thorn was discovered on a mountain top dead by gunshot. He was a well-known author who had written a book on Bill and Hillary Clinton, which revealed their massive corruptions.

**August 2, 2016** – Shawn Lucas was found dead on his bathroom floor by his girlfriend. He had served papers on DNC Debbie Wasserman Shultz for information revealed in Wikileaks e-mails against Bernie Sanders and his religion.

**September 2016** – Hillary Clinton has experienced many suspicious "coughing episodes, head tremors, pill-rolling fingers, strange eye movement, and a body freeze" during her rallies and press speeches. Although many people have requested her health records, as of this date, they have not been fully and truthfully released to the public.

## *Donald J. Trump*

Now that I've presented and discussed only a small fraction of our worldly problems and its evil hidden secrets, we must question together, "What can we possibly do about any of this?"

Mankind's faith is hanging in the balance right now as the control of the **NWO** octopus spreads. On the one hand, we are very close to our complete enslavement, while on the other hand, we could easily crumble to the ground **their pyramid of power**, by simply uniting against their deception in a **peaceful revolution** of minds, hearts and souls. There is one person able to help us do this – Presidential candidate, ***Donald J. Trump*** who may have a low popularity status but I recall something he said at a rally I was watching on TV a few months ago. He said, *"Just think of me as a messenger sent to help America!"*

That may be a strange statement to make, but something which is meaningful. So, we must stop, ponder, and ask ourselves, *"Could God have possibly sent this foul-mouthed, bold, arrogant, rarely compassionate, businessman to really and truly help save America? "*

I believe so. I believe God has granted us a chance in the

next four years to do better than we have done in many decades. Nothing is short of a miracle in this possibility. After all, God has used lesser noble people as a vessel to carry out His plan. Nebuchadnezzar was one of them, if you recall. We must give Mr. Trump some credit for the hard battle he continues to fight. He has *spoken;* but also has seriously *taken* a lot of ugly words from the news media, reporters, television broadcasters, rally protestors and personal families while he bravely defended his image and his rights. Why? I believe people are afraid of him and fear what he might do when and if elected. He is surrounded by a support panel of Evangelicals, military advisors, political counselors, and heaven only knows how many other teams are secretly assisting in closed chambers with the presence of the greatest One of all – GOD! So let's give him credit where credit is now due!

Do you know the reason the establishment elite of Washington hate Donald Trump as they do? Well politically, let's look at the Muslim world which is divided between its two largest camps of distinction – the Sunnis and the Shia. This is the largest and oldest division in the history of Islam. Both of the groups are card-carrying Muslims and Islamists who are very hard-core. Both share a goal for the Middle East and the world to someday be dominated by Islam and Sharia. Although they have differences in doctrine, ritual law, theology and religious organization, they continue in battle to determine which of the two groups will be in charge of the new Islamic world they plan to create. For this reason, they continue fighting and killing each other. However, if someone shows up who is **not** one of them, they will join forces to kill the outsider. This way they have the assurance they will live to run the kingdom.

Similarly, both parties of the Democrats and Republicans have their differences in political doctrine but want the same goal. They are each looking to build a **New World Order** and have dreams of their kingdom on Earth someday. I have mentioned the George Bush family and as well, the Ronald Reagan administration and the Obamas and Clintons, and their affiliations with the Illuminati and secret societies throughout the years. They all share that one dream of being the greatest leader with the most power and money. They will battle with each other, impeach one another, threaten and attempt to outmaneuver each other, lie, cheat, steal until... an outsider comes along and threatens to wipe the entire slate clean and hopefully turn it back over to *We The People of the United States of America.*

What a horrible thought for them to think an outsider could come in and take away their dreams and hopes for wealth and power right out from beneath them. Such an unthinkable idea! I am certain in order to prevent that from happening, they will compromise and negotiate and do deals to let <u>the other side</u> have the power for a while until they can regroup and **try** to take back their territory.
*(Source: In part - CleanTV/Carl Gallups)*

There is no one better than Donald J. Trump to enter their domain and battle with them until he wins. He is the man who Newt Gingrich said, "He can't be controlled or manipulated."

The Illuminati is afraid – if that's possible as powerful as they are – since Mr. Trump does not belong to any secret societies. He could spoil all their plans for a **New World Order.**

Please keep in mind the voting machines can be "rigged" by remote control. It was done by Mike Connell when John Kerry was running against George H.W. Bush. That night in Ohio, Kerry was leading Bush by 3%. Less than an hour later, Bush led Kerry by more than 3%. When Karl Rove asked Mike Connell to take the fall for "rigging the election", he refused. Later, Connell mysteriously crashed his plane into a sand bank and was killed as I have previously mentioned.

Donald J. Trump needs our Christian prayers if he is the one to win this election. There are powerful and evil forces against him. He needs full support from all our evangelicals.

This book is scheduled to be published soon, hopefully before the first or second debates, and much prior to the election. It will be perceived by many as an insult to their party affiliation, their choice of candidate, lifestyles, and expectations for what they believe they want to remain the same – another four years of Obama-life.

In revealing some of the world's secrets, I have been reminded my life could be in jeopardy because their power and money is so great, they could try to take my life. However, I remind those in *evil dominance* that I am clothed in God's righteousness as a born-again Christian and Lucifer cannot touch my **soul**. <u>Jesus is my salvation and I have His coat of armor to protect me.</u>

My heartfelt goal is to reach as many people as possible and have them informed and made aware of the *hidden evil agenda in politics* and the happenings in our world to let them judge for themselves. This is not meant to be party versus party. I don't believe in doing that. Vote for the person! Vote your God-given conscience! Let's work together and help glorify God in making America strong and safe again so He can look down upon us and smile.

# GOD BLESS YOU!
## and
## GOD BLESS AMERICA!

**Presidential Nominee Donald J. Trump.
Will God choose him to win the election,
or will it be someone else?**

*Out of his mouth comes a sharp sword with which to strike down the nations. "He will rule them with an iron scepter." He treads the winepress of the fury of the wrath of God Almighty.* **Revelation 19:15**

**Do you believe Donald actually feels he's a messenger?**

# I DO!

## Final Thoughts from the Author

Oh, my goodness! I'm sure you're pulling at your hair, shaking your head, or jumping up and down after reading all these creepy facts and controversial theories.

I want to thank those who contributed articles, which I carefully researched for intelligibility, proficiency, and reason. It is worth remembering that in any philosophy (theory), there is fact and substance, even if it seems inexplicable.

We live in a "bubble" protected by family, friends, and our church. We do not see the *"outside world"* as it revolves around **evil**. We really do not want to see it in that horrendous form. Therefore, we have chosen to **not** acknowledge the likelihood of what is really happening in this devious and dark world of mystery, lies, and deception.

The greed for authority and power over others with the love of money from wars, suffering, and death is the evil vindication Satan continues to target for the family of Christ. He and his demonic angels will stop at nothing to inflict pain during his rebellion throughout the universe of all people. This evil destruction will not end until *Jesus* returns to Earth.

I leave you with the truth that *Jesus Christ* loves you and is willing to forgive you of all your sins – past, present, and future sins that are a disease of the human heart. There is no other way of salvation except through *Jesus* and the cross. In closing, I would like to ask you to put your trust in *Christ* and say this prayer:

*"Dear Heavenly Father, I know that I'm a sinner. I ask for Your forgiveness. I believe that You died for my sins, and You rose from the dead. I turn from my sin. I repent of my sins. I invite You to come into my heart and life. I want to trust and follow You as my personal Lord and Savior. In Jesus' Name, I pray. Amen."*

For God so loved the world, that He gave His only begotten Son, that whosoever believeth in Him should not perish, but have everlasting life. John 3:16

This is His Grace...

## Christian Published Author
# Jeanie Cline

## Other Books by this Author

*Step Into My Heart*
*Ancient of Days*
*A Winter's Season*
*Sunrise in Deer Hollow*
*Two Rooms*
*When Love is Enough*
*Great is thy Faithfulness*
*Our Childhood at East Harper School*
*Pitch Perfect in the 50's*
*Christmas in Lenoir in the 50's*
*Following God's Steps to Israel*